BT/09 .H35

Property of
INSTITUTE FOR WORSHIP STUDIES
Orange Park, Florida

PHOTIUS AND THE CAROLINGIANS
THE TRINITARIAN CONTROVERSY

PHOTIUS
AND
THE CAROLINGIANS
The Trinitarian Controversy

RICHARD HAUGH

NORDLAND PUBLISHING COMPANY
BELMONT, MASSACHUSSETTS 02178

BY THE SAME AUTHOR

Aleksandr Solzhenitsyn: Critical Essays and Documentary Materials [co-edited with John B. Dunlop and Alexis Klimoff] 1973

Library of Congress Catalog Card Number 74-22859
ISBN 0-913124-05-2

© Copyright 1975 by NORDLAND PUBLISHING COMPANY

All Rights Reserved

PRINTED IN THE UNITED STATES OF AMERICA

DEDICATED WITH GRATITUDE TO

FR. JOHN MEYENDORFF
PROFESSOR SERGE VERHOVSKOY

AND TO THE MEMORY OF

HERBERT MUSURILLO, S.J.

"If you reject the Middle Ages, the history of the West collapses, and the rest of modern history becomes incomprehensible..."

                Ol'da Andozerskaia
                in Solzhenitsyn's *August 1914*
                [p. 548]

"The Photian case is not merely a matter of Byzantine interest. It concerns the history of Christianity and of the world, as the appraisement of Photius and his work lies at the core of the controversies that separate the Eastern and the Western Churches."

                Francis Dvornik
                The Photian Schism
                [p. 15]

Perhaps it is in the reign of Charlemagne that the schism of civilizations first becomes clearly apparent."

                Timothy Ware
                The Orthodox Church
                [p. 54]

About the Author

Dr. Richard Haugh is Adjunct Professor in the Department of Classics and Assistant Professor of Religious Studies at Iona College, New Rochelle, New York. Translator of various works from German, French, and Latin and author of articles on Dostoevsky, Solzhenitsyn, Carolingian thought, Patristics, and Old Norse literature, Dr. Haugh is co-editor (with John B. Dunlop of Oberlin College and Alexis Klimoff of Vassar College) of *Aleksandr Solzhenitsyn: Critical Essays and Documentary Materials*. He is an editor of the annual scholarly journal *Transactions of the Association of Russian-American Scholars*.

Acknowledgments

I would like to express my gratitude to Fr. John Meyendorff for the time he so generously gave me. I gratefully acknowledge my theological debt to Professor Serge Verhovskoy of St. Vladimir's Theological Seminary. I also wish to thank Maria-Pompea Pellicciari for translating the valuable research of Vittorio Peri on the "shields" of Pope Leo III from Italian for me. Raymond Ciuba also worked with me on the translation of the *Epistola Peregrinorum Monachorum*.

A special gratitude is owed to the late scholar Fr. Herbert Musurillo, S.J. It was he who suggested the publication of this work.

If it had not been for the selfless sacrifices of my wife Vera, this work would have never been written.

R. HAUGH

The Elevation of The Cross
September 14, 1974

Contents

Preface 13-14

Chapter I
The Theological and Historical Problem 15-21
    The Latin Triadological Model/The Greek Triadological Model/The Carolingians and the Hermeneutical Problem/The Carolingians and the Historical Problem

Chapter II
The Historical Preparation for the Crisis 23-44
    The *Filioque* and the Post-Augustinian West/The Ecumenical Creed/The Council of Toledo (589)/The Anglo-Saxon Church and the *Filioque*/Rome and the *Filioque*/Cultural Estrangement/Political Estrangement/The Council of Gentilly

Chapter III
The *Libri Carolini* 45-53

Chapter IV
Paulinus of Aquileia and Alcuin 55-62
    The Council of Friuli/Alcuin

Chapter V
The Jerusalem Controversy and Its Aftermath 63-77
    The Letter of the Pilgrim Monks/Pope Leo's Letter to the Eastern Churches/Theodulf's *De Spiritu Sancto*/*Libellus de Processione Spiritus Sancti*

Chapter VI
The Frankish Envoys and Pope Leo III 79-90
    Smaragdus' Letter to Pope Leo III/The Meeting Between the Franks and Pope Leo III

Chapter VII
Photius' *Encyclical* 91-99
    The Christianization of the Slavs/The *Encyclical*

Chapter VIII

The Latin Response to Photius' *Encyclical* 101-121
   The Response of Pope Nicholas/The Response of Aeneas of Paris/The Response of Ratramnus of Corbie/The Response of the Council of Worms

Chapter IX

The Photian Council of 879-880 123-130
   Byzantine Internal Problems/The Council of 879-880/Pope John's Letter to Photius

Chapter X

Photius' Letter to the Patriarch of Aquileia 131-139

Chapter XI

Photius' *Mystagogia* 141-157
   The Theological Critique of the *Filioque*/The Response to Carolingian Exegesis/Photius and the Latin Fathers/Photius and the Roman Popes/The Roman Popes and the Creed/The Creed as Perfect/Photius' Conclusion

Chapter XII

Conclusions 159-177
   Historical Conclusions/Theological Conclusions

Appendix:

The Patristic Background 179-205
   I. Introductory Background
   II. The Greek Patristic Background: Athanasius/Didymus the Blind/The Cappadocian Fathers/Cyril of Alexandria
   III. The Latin Patristic Background: Hilary of Poitiers/Ambrose/Augustine

Bibliography 207-214

List of Roman Popes 215

List of Patriarchs of Constantinople 217

List of Roman [Byzantine] Emperors 219

List of "German" "Roman" Emperors................221

Index 223

Preface

This study was begun in 1968 when the author was in his last year of M.A. studies at Andover Newton Theological School and it was essentially completed in 1973 when the author was in his last year of doctoral studies at Fordham University.

This work, the first part of a projected study of the history of the "Trinitarian Controversy" up to the present, attempts to explore and analyze a vitally important area of historical theology which in the past has been either cursorily referred to, or treated from a biased Western perspective, or simply ignored.

Historically the question of the procession of the Holy Spirit has been one of the most significant controversies in the history of Christian thought, a controversy which concerns the heart of the Christian vision of God. The conclusion of this first volume is that the Carolingian period, unsophisticated as it may be, was *the* decisive formative stage in the history of a problem which later became an insurmountable barrier between the Eastern and Western Churches. This volume attempts to determine the historical sequence of the Carolingian-Byzantine Trinitarian controversy and presents and analyzes the comparative theological presuppositions of the Carolingians and the Byzantines.

The most important section of the Appendix is the

analysis of the triadological thought of Augustine and Cyril of Alexandria. The rest of the Appendix exists only as a short "frame of reference" to those "Fathers" whom the Carolingians use as "patristic authorities."

The triadological thought of John Scotus Eriugena (d.c. 877) has been deliberately excluded from this volume precisely because his triadological thought was in no way involved in the *controversy* between the East and West. In general the thought of John Scotus Eriugena was not much appreciated in the Latin West, especially his participation in the internal Carolingian controversy on predestination. John Scotus Eriugena had the distinction of having his thought condemned at most of the important councils in the Latin West, especially in 855[1] and 859. His thought was condemned as *"pultes scotarum."* His thought on the procession of the Holy Spirit was no more appreciated than his thought on other subjects, for he shared the Eastern Christian position that the Holy Spirit proceeds from the Father *through* the Son.[2]

The "dogmatization" of the *Filioque* by the Latin West at the Second Council of Lyons in 1274 will be discussed at length in the second volume of this study. One point, however, must be stressed. It was at this Council of Lyons that the Latin West first dogmatically presented the *Filioque* as *"Ex Patre Filioque Tanquam Ab Uno Principio."* As soon as one begins to approach the *Filioque* as *"Ab Uno Principio,"* the very nature of the problem changes, for there is now no reality to the *"que."* The earlier controversy therefore changes its nature. But such a formulation by the Latin West proves one of Photius' main points—the Latin West did in fact, as Photius charged, envision the procession of the Holy Spirit in a de-personalized manner, ultimately rooting its vision of God in "nature" or "essence." Photius' charges actually take on *more* significance in the light of this later dogmatic definition.

---

[1]The Council of Valence in 855 condemned nineteen aspects of the thought of John Scotus Eriugena: *"... sed et alia 19 syllogismis ineptissime conclusa..."*

[2]See *De Divisione Naturae,* Book II, 30 and 32 (*PL* 122).

CHAPTER I

The Theological and Historical Problem

The doctrinal aspect of the Byzantine-Carolingian Triadological controversy centers primarily on one issue. Does the Holy Spirit proceed; that is, take his very existence, from the Father *or* from the Father and the Son. In their attack on Byzantine triadology the Carolingian theologians constantly appeal to the "authority" of certain Church Fathers[1] to support their position that the Holy Spirit derives his existence from the Father and the Son.

That the question of the procession of the Holy Spirit was already controversial in the Latin West in the fourth century is evident from statements by Hilary of Poitiers,[2]

---

[1] The Carolingian patristic appeal restricts itself primarily to Athanasius, Cyril of Alexandria, Didymus the Blind, Gregory of Nazianzus, Hilary, Ambrose, Augustine and numerous post-Augustinian Latin theologians. See the appendix for an analysis of the triadological thought of these Fathers to whom the Carolingian theologians appeal.

[2] In his *De Trinitate* VIII, 20 (J. P. Migne, *Patrologia Latina* [Paris, 1844-1855], 10, 250; hereafter cited as *PL*) Hilary attests to the fact that

Ambrose,[3] and Augustine.[4]

Two triadological "models" emerged from the fourth century; one was the Greek "model" shaped primarily by the Cappadocian Fathers; the other was the Latin "model" shaped by Augustine.[5]

The Latin Triadological Model

In structuring the Latin triadological "model," Augustine begins with the inseparable oneness of the Divine Essence and only later considers the personal existence of the Trinity. Augustine's starting point is the oneness of God in whom there are three Persons. The doctrine of the procession of the Spirit from the Father and the Son follows rather logically from Augustine's perspective of God. Augustine developed his Filioque theology in his *De Trinitate* and became more explicit about this teaching in his *Tractatus in Joannis Evangelium* and in his *Contra Maximinum Arianum*.

Augustine's support for the doctrine of the *Filioque* will be repeated again and again by the Carolingian theologians. Augustine concludes that since the Spirit is the Spirit "of the Son," then the Spirit must proceed from the Son. Since the Spirit is sent by the Son, he must therefore

---

the procession of the Spirit was controversial. He writes: "For the present I allow *their* freedom of speculation, *some* of them holding that the Paraclete Spirit comes from the Father or from the Son."

[3]In his *De Spiritu Sancto* I, 152-154 (*PL* 16, 769) Ambrose writes: "*Many* have declared that the Son is also signified as the Fountain of Life; that is, the Fountain of the Holy Spirit . . . Yet *many* wish that the Father alone be indicated in this passage..."

[4]In the ninth chapter of his *De fide et symbolo* (*PL* 40, 181-196) Augustine acknowledges that there were various "parties" on this subject.

[5]See the Appendix for an analysis of Augustinian triadology.

proceed from the Son. Since Christ breathed the Spirit on his disciples, the Spirit obviously proceeds from the Son. Since the Holy Spirit is the common bond, the union of love, between the Father and the Son, he must proceed from both. Since the Son has "all" things which the Father has, he must also have the power, given to him from the Father, which causes the Spirit to proceed from him; that is, to come into existence from the Son also.

Augustine became the most authoritative Church Father for the Carolingian theologians.[6] Although all the Carolingian theologians who were involved in the Triadological controversy quote at length from Augustine, some Carolingian theologians, especially Ratramnus of Corbie, not only quoted from Augustine but also thoroughly mastered the theological content of Augustinian triadology.

The Greek Triadological Model

The Greek triadological "model" begins not with the oneness of the Divine Essence but with the personal reality of God the Father, the Personal source of all life, uncreated and created. If God the Father is the source [ἡ ἀρχή] of all existence, then he is also the source and the cause of the life of the Holy Spirit. Since God the Father is perfect, the way (procession) in which the Holy Spirit comes forth from the Father must also be perfect. If the procession of the Spirit from the Father is perfect, then the Son can in no way be a cause of the existence of

---

[6]Hans von Schubert is quite accurate in assessing Carolingian theology: "Der Traditionalismus ist noch immer die Signatur der Zeit und zwar ist mehr als je der grosse abendländischen Denker zum Kirchenvater geworden, Augustin . . . die Schriften des Afrikaners (waren) ein gewaltiges Arsenal." Hans von Schubert, *Geschichte der christlichen Kirche im Frühmittelalter* (Tübingen, 1921), p. 377.

the Holy Spirit. The Holy Spirit may indeed proceed eternally from the Father through the Son but, according to the Greek triadological "model," the Spirit does not derive his existence from the Son. Hence, from within the perspective of the Greek triadological "model" the Latin *interpretation* of the *Filioque* is theologically incompatible.

According to the deepest insight of the Greek triadological "model," God the Father is the Father of the Son precisely because in the depth of the ontology of love the Father has an image of himself because he perfectly knows himself. But the perfection of this knowledge only personally "perfects" itself—to stretch human language—when it is known hypostatically; that is, in another Person.[7] Consistent with the ontology of love and perfection, God the Father cannot limit himself to himself. Rather, perfect existence seeks to spread its existence to others.[8] Hence, the simultaneous parallel acts of the begetting of the Son as the personal image of the Father and the procession of the Spirit as the personal life and holiness of the Father.

The pattern of the Greek triadological "model" was succinctly summarized by John Damascene (d. c. 749).

> [We believe] in one Father, the principle and cause [ἡ ἀρχή] of everything . . . Father of only one by nature, his Only-Begotten Son . . . and Projector [προβολή] of the most Holy Spirit . . . The Holy Spirit proceeds from the Father . . . For this is the teaching of Holy Scripture . . . We also believe in the Holy Spirit . . . who proceeds from the Father and rests in the Son . . . proceeding from the Father and communicated through the Son . . . the begetting of the Son and the procession of the Holy Spirit are simultaneous . . . Therefore, all that the Son and Spirit have is from the Father, including their very existence. Unless the Father exists, neither the Son nor Spirit exists. And unless the Father possesses a specific quality, neither the Son nor Spirit can possess it . . . *We do not speak of the Son as Cause* . . . We speak of

---

[7]The term *hypostasis* is used throughout in the sense of person.

[8]The idea that Person cannot be satisfied with self-existence, and the significance of this for triadological thought, was perceived by Richard of St. Victor in his *De Trinitate* III (PL 196, 915-930).

the Holy Spirit as from the Father and call him the Spirit of the Father. And we do not speak of the Spirit as from the Son, although we call him the Spirit of the Son.⁹

The Carolingians and the Hermeneutical Problem

In working with the texts of the Greek Fathers, the Carolingian theologians confront a significant hermeneutical problem. Many of the texts of the Greek Fathers, when taken out of the context of the perspective of the Greek triadological "model," can be interpreted to support the Latin teaching of the procession of the Spirit from the Father and the Son. For example, the Greek Fathers never deny the Biblical fact that the Spirit is the "Spirit of the Son." For the Greek East this was interpreted as a proof of the Spirit's consubstantiality with the Son. For the Carolingian theologians, interpreting this expression from within the perspective of the Latin triadological "model" and relying on the earlier Biblical exegesis of Augustine, the very existence of such an expression in the Greek Fathers was interpreted as a proof that the Greek Fathers also taught that the Spirit proceeds from the Son.

Quite often the Greek Fathers speak of the Holy Trinity in its "economic" activity; that is, in its relation to creation and salvation. For example, the Alexandrian theologians, especially Athanasius and Cyril,[10] seldom speak of the inner life and eternal relations of the Holy Trinity. Their many expressions which speak of the Spirit coming from or through the Son almost always refer to the temporal mission of the Spirit and not the Spirit's eternal procession. The Carolingian theologians, however, do not distinguish

---

[9]*De Fide Orthodoxa* I, 8 [J. P. Migne, *Patrologia Graeca* (Paris, 1857-1866), 94, 805ff.; hereafter cited as *PG*].

[10]See the Appendix for an analysis of Cyril's thought.

between the temporal mission and the eternal procession of the Spirit. Thus, whenever they confront texts of the Greek Fathers which refer to the temporal mission of the Spirit, they interpret these texts as a proof that the Greek Fathers taught that the Spirit proceeds from the Son. Hermeneutically the original meaning of these expressions was lost.

The Carolingians and the Historical Problem

The hermeneutical problem is inextricably bound up with a larger historical problem which is essentially two-fold. First, quite often the Carolingian theologians quote from works which were spurious. The most significant example of this is the Carolingian appeal to Athanasius. Whenever they appeal to Athanasius, the Carolingian theologians primarily quote from the pseudo-Athanasian corpus, thinking in good faith that these were the authentic works of Athanasius. The pseudo-Athanasian corpus includes the *De Incarnatione contra Apollinarem*,[11] the *Sermo maior de fide*,[12] the *Expositio fidei*,[13] the *Interpretatio in symbolum*,[14] the *Dialogi contra Macedonianos*,[15] the *Dialogi de sancta Trinitate quinque*,[16] the *De Trinitate Libri XII*,[17] and the truly remark-

---

[11] *PG* 26, 1093-1166.
[12] *PG* 26, 1263-1294.
[13] *PG* 25, 199-208.
[14] *PG* 26, 1231-1232.
[15] *PG* 28, 1291-1338.
[16] *PG* 28, 1115-1286.
[17] *PL* 62, 237-334. These "represent a collection of treatises by several unknown authors of the West, who composed them approximately in the second half of the fourth and in the fifth century." Johannes Quasten, *Patrology* (3 vols.; Westminster Press, 1950-1960), III, 33-34.

ably influential *Symbolum Athanasianum*.[18] Whenever the Carolingian theologians quote from the authentic works of Athanasius, they conclude from his stress on the inseparability and consubstantiality of the Divine Persons that the Spirit must therefore proceed from the Son.

Secondly, the Carolingian theologians were "prisoners of history." The Latin triadological "model" with its concomitant doctrine of the *Filioque* and its concomitant methodology of Biblical exegesis had become so firmly entrenched in the Latin West, especially in the Germanic territories, that the Carolingians were to a great extent historically determined. However, these "prisoners of history" ultimately became the "architects of history."

---

[18]*PL* 88, 585f.

CHAPTER II

The Historical Preparation For the Crisis

Several events prepared the way for the Byzantine-Carolingian Triadological controversy. The *Filioque* presented a theological and a canonical problem. The theological problem was the doctrine of the *Filioque* itself; the canonical problem concerned itself with the addition of the *Filioque* to the Ecumenical Creed. Although the two are separate problems, they became united under the Carolingian theologians. While *Filioque* theology entrenched itself in the Latin West, political and cultural problems brought about a separation of the Latin West and the Byzantine East, a separation which reached a critical point during the Carolingian era.

The Filioque and the Post-Augustinian West

After Augustine the Latin West seemed to accept the doctrine of the *Filioque* as a matter of course. Almost all the Latin theological writers,¹ even those who vigorously opposed Augustinian thought in other areas, expressed a belief in the *doctrine* of the *Filioque,* providing the Carolingian theologians a host of "authorities" to support their position. Some considered the *Filioque* as a doctrine taught by the universal Church. Julianus Pomerius (d. 498) of Arles, for example, claimed that the doctrine should be taught to all the faithful.² Fulgentius of Ruspe (d. c. 533), a thorough Augustinian on all issues, wrote with assurance that the doctrine had apostolic sanction.³ And Cassiodorus (d. c. 580) claimed it as the teaching of "Mother Church."⁴

While they had no tendency to add the *Filioque* to the Ecumenical Creed, certain Roman Popes⁵ after Augustine

---

¹Eucherius (d. 453) of Lyons, *Instructionibus ad Salonium* (*PL* 50, 774); Faustus (d. 485) of Riez, *De Spiritu Sancto* 1, 1, 10 (*PL* 62, 21); Gennadius (d. 495) of Marseilles, *De ecclesiasticus dogmatibus* (*PL* 58, 980); Vigilius (d. 520) of Thapsus, *Contra Eutychetem* I, 10 (*PL* 62, 101); Paschasius (d. 512), deacon of Rome, *De Spiritu Sancto* 1, 12 (*PL* 62, 23); Boethius (d. 524), *De Trinitate* 5 (*PL* 64, 1254); Fulgentius (d. 533), Bishop of Ruspe, *De Trinitate* II (*PL* 65, 499) and *Epistola* 14, 28 (*PL* 65, 373); Fulgentius Ferrandus (d. 546), *Epistola 7 ad Reginum* 12 (*PL* 67, 940); Agnellus (d. 569) of Ravenna, *Epistola ad Armenum de ratione fidei* (*PL* 68, 383); Rusticus, deacon of Rome, *Disputatione contra Acephalos* (*PL* 67, 1237). Rusticus, nephew of Pope Vigilius (537-555), wrote that he had doubts on the subject of the procession of the Holy Spirit, although his doubt seems to be not that the Holy Spirit proceeds from the Son, but how he proceeds from the Son: ". . . ego vero quia Spiritus quidem Filium non genuerit sempiterne confiteor . . . utrum vero a Filio eodem modo quo a Patre procedat, *nondum perfecte satisfactum habeo."*

²See *De Vita contemplativa* 1, 1, 18 (*PL* 59, 432). Avitus (d. 523), Archbishop of Vienne, believed the *Filioque* was catholic; see *Fragmentis Epistolae de divinitate Spiritus Sancti* (*PL* 59, 385).

³"De Filio quoque procedere Spiritum Sanctum, prophetica atque *apostolica* nobis *doctrina* commendat." (*PL* 65, 696).

⁴"O vere sancta, o immaculata, o perfecta *mater ecclesia,* cujus piae confessioni nihil addi, nihil minui potest . . . Patrem . . . docens ingenitum, Filium genitum, Spiritum Sanctum de Patre et Filio procedentem." (*PL* 70, 23).

⁵There is a strong possibility that Pope Leo's (d. 461) letter to Turibius is authentic (See *Epistola* 15; *PL* 54, 678). In Pope Leo's Sermon on Pentecost a belief in the *Filioque* is implicit (See *Sermo 75, De Pentecoste*

expressed a belief in the procession of the Spirit from the Father and the Son. One of the Popes most often quoted by the Carolingian theologians was Pope Gregory the Great (d. 604)[6] whose homilies were quite popular with the Carolingians.

The Ecumenical Creed

Although the Ecumenical Creed of the First Ecumenical Council at Nicaea (325) simply stated: "And [we believe] in the Holy Spirit," the Second Ecumenical Council at Constantinople (381) expanded the section of the Ecumenical Creed on the Holy Spirit to: "And in the Holy Spirit, the Lord and the Giver-of-Life, who proceeds from the Father, who together with the Father and the Son is worshipped and glorified..."[7] The Carolingian theologians Paulinus of Aquileia and Ratramnus of Corbie will refer to this "addition" to the original Nicene Creed as support for the later "addition" of the *Filioque.*

Although it is true that the Third Ecumenical Council at Ephesus (431) prohibited any creed which opposed the established Nicene Creed,[8] the Fourth Ecumenical Council at

---

1, 3; *PL* 54, 678). The authenticity of Pope Hormisdas' (d. 523) *Epistola ad Iustinum imperatorem* (*PL* 63, 514) is questionable.

[6]That Pope Gregory accepted the belief in the procession of the Spirit from the Son appears undeniable. See *Homilia 26 in Evangelia* 2; *PL* 75, 1198; *Moralium* 1, 30, 4; *PL* 76, 533 f.; and *Moralium* 1, 22; *PL* 76, 541.

[7]J. D. Mansi, *Sacrorum conciliorum nova et amplissima collectio* (Florence and Venice, 1759 ff.), 3, 565; hereafter cited as Mansi. (The English translation, slightly altered, is from volume XIV of the second series of *Nicene and Post-Nicene Fathers,* ed. by Schaff and Wace (28 vols.; Buffalo, 1886-1900), p. 163; hereafter cited as *NPNF*).

[8]See Canon VII; *NPNF* XIV, p. 231.

Chalcedon (451) is quite explicit in referring to the Nicene-Constantinopolitan—not the Nicene—Creed:

> . . . the Holy Ecumenical Synod defines that no one shall be permitted to bring forward a different faith [ἑτέραν πίστιν], nor to write, nor to put together, nor to excogitate, nor to teach it to others. But such as dare either to put together another faith, or to bring forward or to teach or to deliver a different Creed [ἕτερον σύμβολον] . . . if they be Bishops or clerics let them be deposed . . . if they be monks or laics: let them be anathematized.[9]

The Nicene-Constantinopolitan Ecumenical Creed was not, however, the only creed in circulation. Formularies, professions of faith, and various creeds circulated along with the Nicene-Constantinopolitan Creed without in any way attempting to challenge the ecumenicity of the One Creed of the Universal Church. The most important of these other creeds, and the most efficacious in entrenching the *Filioque* in the Latin West, was the *Quicunque,* falsely attributed to Athanasius and also known as the Athanasian Creed.[10]

The trinitarian section (articles 1-28) of the lengthy *Quicunque* is thoroughly Augustinian in content. Concerning the Holy Spirit it states: "The Holy Spirit is from the Father and the Son, not made, nor created, nor begotten, but proceeding."[11] After its section on the Holy Trinity, the *Quicunque* states: "So he who wishes to be saved should think thus of the Trinity." Indeed, the *Quicunque* creed claims to be the faith of the universal Church.[12]

The *Quicunque*, a compendium of Augustinian triadology

---

[9]See *NPNF* XIV, p. 265.

[10]*Symbolum Athanasianum* (*PL* 88, 585 f.).

[11]"Spiritus Sanctus a Patre et Filio, non factus, nec creatus, nec genitus, sed procedens." That this refers to the eternal procession of the Holy Spirit is clear from the preceding text which states that the "Son is from the Father *alone,* not made, nor created, but begotten."

[12]The *Quicunque Creed begins* with: "Whoever desires to be saved must above all things hold the Catholic faith. Unless a man keeps it in its entirety inviolate, he will assuredly perish eternally. Now this is the Catholic faith." The creed ends in the same manner.

along with other texts from Vincent of Lérins, seems to have originated in southern Gaul about the year 500.[13] Although the author still remains unknown, much of the evidence points to the monastery of Lérins and perhaps to the sponsorship of Caesarius of Arles (d. 543), who is the earliest witness of the creed, according to the important discovery by G. Morin in 1931 of a manuscript containing Caesarius' sermons. A statement from the preface is noteworthy:

> And because it is necessary, and incumbent on them, that all clergymen, and laymen too, should be familiar with the Catholic faith, we have first of all written out in this collection the Catholic faith itself as the holy fathers defined it, for we ought both ourselves frequently to read it and to instruct others in it.[14]

The Catholic Faith which then follows is the *Quicunque Creed*. Thereafter the *Quicunque* works its way into individual theology, into professions of faith, and into the conciliar decrees of Spanish councils. Soon the *Filioque* theology of the *Quicunque Creed* transfers itself to the Ecumenical Creed by adding the *Filioque* to the original text.

The Council of Toledo (589)

In 589 at the national Spanish Council of Toledo, presided over by Isidore of Seville's elder brother Leander, the Visigoths, led by their King Reccared, renounced Arianism and accepted "catholic" Christianity. The Spanish theologians, having suffered at length from the heresies of an Arianism tainted with the ideas of Macedonius and a

---

[13]See J. N. D. Kelly, *The Athanasian Creed* (London, 1964), pp. 35-48; 109-127 and G. Morin, "L'Origine du symbole d'Athanase," *Revue Bénédictine*, XLIV (1932), 207-219.

[14]Quoted from Kelly, *op. cit.*, p. 36.

Priscillianism tainted with the ideas of Sabellius, believed that with the *Filioque* they were both asserting the Catholic faith and protecting the Divine consubstantiality of the Son. Indeed, they were not even conscious of altering the Nicene-Constantinopolitan Creed.

In his opening speech to the council King Reccared declared that "the Holy Spirit also should be confessed by us and taught to proceed from the Father and the Son."[15] His clergy was then ordered to remain loyal to the faith. Then, after professing his acceptance of the first Four Ecumenical Councils, he recites both the Nicene and the Nicene-Constantinopolitan Creeds, the latter with the *Filioque* addition. Ironically, even the definitions of the Fourth Ecumenical Council prohibiting any alteration of the Creed were appended to this Spanish council.

There are twenty-three anathemas declared by this council, the third of which "anathematizes those who do not profess that the Holy Spirit proceeds from the Father and the Son."[16] Again ironically, the eleventh anathema is against those who do not accept the decrees of the first Four Ecumenical Councils.[17] By his kingly authority Reccared also decreed that

> all the churches of Spain and Gallica, in order to give support to the recent conversion of his people, should observe this rule: that is, at every sacrifice, before receiving the body or blood of Christ, the most holy symbol of the faith should be recited in a loud voice by all, *according to the custom of the Eastern Fathers*.[18]

---

[15]Mansi 9, 978.

[16]Mansi 9, 985.

[17]Mansi 9, 985: "Quicumque aliam fidem et communionem catholicam, praeter ecclesiasticam universalem, esse crediderit, (illam dicimus ecclesiam, quae Nicaeni, Constantinopolitani, et primi Ephesini, et Chalcedonensis concilii decreta tenet pariter et honorat) anathema sit." See also anathema XX, XXI, and XXII (9,987).

[18]Mansi 9, 990: ". . . *juxta orientalium patrum morem* unanimiter clara voce sacratissimum fidei recenseant symbolum. . ."

Of the twenty-three canons issued by this Spanish council the second is noteworthy:

> in all the churches of Spain and Gallica, the symbol of the faith of the Council of Constantinople, that is, of the 150 Fathers, be recited *according to the form of the Eastern Churches*, so that it be chanted in a loud voice by the people before the Lord's prayer is said.[19]

It is strikingly clear that the Council of Toledo did not consciously alter the Ecumenical Creed. They obviously believed that the *Filioque* was included in the original Nicene-Constantinopolitan Creed. The *Filioque,* both as doctrine and as found in various creedal statements and professions of faith, had so firmly rooted itself in the Latin West after Augustine that its authenticity and authority were simply taken for granted. After the Council of Toledo in 589 the *Filioque* was zealously propagated in Spain by individuals,[20] by Spanish councils,[21] and through liturgical texts.[22]

The *Filioque* development in Spain is of utmost importance for the Carolingian theological tradition, because one of the most important Carolingian theologians, Theodulf of Orléans, quite probably the main author of the monumental *Libri Carolini,* came to Charlemagne's court from Spain, bringing with him this Spanish tradition of both *Filioque* doctrine and the interpolated Ecumenical Creed.

---

[19]Mansi 9, 992 f. At Constantinople the Ecumenical Creed was first inserted in the Eucharistic Liturgy by Patriarch Timothy I (511-518), according to Theodorus Lector. See *PG* 86, 201 f. According to the same source, it is possible that at Antioch the Creed found its way into the Liturgy about 471. See *PG* 86, 209.

[20]The Spanish theologian most often quoted by the Carolingian theologians is Isidore of Seville (d. 636). For Isidore's *Filioque* theology see his *Etymologiarum* (*PL* 82, 268 and 271) and his *Sententiarum* (*PL* 83, 568).

[21]At the 4th (633), 6th (638), 8th (655), 11th (675), 12th (681), 13th (683), 14th (688), 15th (688), 16th (693) and 17th (694) Councils of Toledo, at the Council of Merida (663) and at the Council of Braga (675).

[22]See the prayers of the Gothic Breviary for vespers and matins of Pentecost (*PL* 86, 691 and *PL* 85, 612).

The Anglo-Saxon Church and the Filioque

The background of *Filioque* theology in the Anglo-Saxon church is important for the Carolingian period because another influential Carolingian theologian, Alcuin, brings this tradition with him to the court of Charlemagne.

Although there is no evidence that the *Filioque* was inserted in the Ecumenical Creed in England, *Filioque* theology had penetrated there also. In September of 680 the Anglo-Saxon Bishops gathered at Hatfield. This most significant council was presided over by Theodore of Tarsus, a Greek from Asia Minor, who, while visiting in Rome, was asked by Pope Vitalian (657-672) to go to England as the Archbishop of Canterbury in order to organize the Anglo-Saxon church. This council,[23] after professing adherence to the first Five Ecumenical Councils, stated:

> . . . and we glorify our Lord Jesus Christ, as *they* glorified him, neither adding nor diminishing anything; anathematizing those with our hearts and mouths whom *they* anathematized, and receiving those whom *they* received, glorifying God the Father, who is without beginning, and his only begotten Son generated from eternity, and the Holy Spirit proceeding from the Father and the Son in an ineffable manner, as *those* holy apostles, prophets, and doctors, whom we have above-mentioned, did declare. And all we, who, with Archbishop Theodore, have thus expounded the Catholic faith, have also subscribed thereto.[24]

Thus the English council, presided over by the Greek Theodore, believed that the procession of the Spirit from the Father and the Son was apostolic. There is no reason to dismiss this as a later interpolation, for one should not be surprised that *Filioque* theology and *Filioque* expressions entered England. How and when this occurred is unknown,

---

[23] The source is the Venerable Bede (d. 735), *Historia Ecclesiastica Gentis Anglorum* (Mansi 11, 176).

[24] The English translation is from *Ecclesiastical History of the English Nation* (New York: Dutton, 1963), p. 192.

although the *Filioque* could easily have been brought to England by Augustine of Canterbury (d. 605), a disciple of Pope Gregory the Great. What is surprising is that Theodore signed such a statement of faith. However, Theodore perhaps realized it would be futile to oppose such an entrenched Latin tradition. And, indeed, Theodore himself was being watched. When Pope Vitalian sent Theodore to England, he sent with Theodore an African theologian named Hadrian with the express purpose of preventing Theodore from introducing any Greek customs into the English church.[25] Although Pope Vitalian's suspicion of Greek "customs" at this time concerned Monothelite Christology, any Greek "custom" differing from Latin tradition would probably have evoked controversy.

Rome and the Filioque

It must not be thought that the entire Latin West accepted the two-fold problem of the *Filioque* so readily. In Italy even those who accepted the *doctrine* of the *Filioque* were intransigently opposed to any insertion of it in the Ecumenical Creed.

A profession of faith issued by the Council of Milan in 680 expressed a belief in the procession of the Spirit from the Person of the Father.[26] And at Rome in 680 Pope Agatho (678-681) convoked a council attended by 125 Western Bishops which resulted in the sending of two letters to the Emperor of Constantinople, both letters written in the name of Pope Agatho. The first letter stated that "we

---

[25] Bede, *op. cit.*, IV, 1: "The Pope also ordered Hadrian to give full support to Theodore in his teaching, and to watch that he did not introduce into the Church over which he was to rule any Greek customs [*Graecorum more*] which conflicted with the teaching of the true Faith."

[26] Mansi 11, 206.

guard with sincerity of heart the faith which our fathers have left us, supplicating of God, as our greatest good, to preserve both the meaning and the words of their decisions without any kind of addition, subtraction or alteration."[27] In the second and most interesting letter Pope Agatho professed

> to guard in closest keeping of our mind the definitions of the Catholic and Apostolic faith, which the Apostolic throne has both kept and hands down to the present, believing in one God, the Father Almighty . . . and the Holy Spirit . . . who proceeds from the Father.[28]

The explicitness of Pope Agatho's confession may have been prompted by a preceding controversy which involved Pope Martin I (649-655). "Once at least in the seventh century, during the heat of the Monothelite controversy, there was a foretaste of the stir the Latin doctrine of the Procession was destined to make in the Greek East at a later time."[29] Constantinople accused Pope Martin of believing that the Spirit proceeds from the Father and the Son, a statement the Pope allegedly wrote in a synodical letter. Knowledge of this event comes from a fragment of a letter by Maximus the Confessor to the priest Marinus.[30]

If this letter is authentic,[31] which is here assumed, it is

---

[27]Mansi 11, 235-238.

[28]Mansi 11, 289 f. "Credentes in Deum Patrem . . . et in Spiritum sanctum, dominum et vivificatorem, ex Patre procedentem..."

[29]Swete, *The Holy Spirit in the Ancient Church* (London, 1912), p. 279.

[30]*Epistola ad Marinum, Cypri presbyterum* (PG 91, 133 ff.).

[31]Reasons for doubting the authenticity of this letter are: (1) Maximus himself mentions a spurious letter to Marinus which was attributed to him (PG 91, 129); (2) there is no extant synodical letter by Pope Martin with such an expression; and (3) the letter speaks of "six" councils when only five had at that time been held. The first and second objections are not serious, for Maximus may have been referring to another letter and the fact that Pope Martin's letter is not extant does not mean that it did not exist. The reference to "six" councils, however, presents a problem. It is possible that Maximus was referring to the Lateran council

most noteworthy. Maximus writes that the "synodical letter of the present Pope" was challenged by Constantinople on two issues, one of which concerned the Pope's statement that "the Holy Spirit proceeds also from the Son." When Maximus questioned the Latins about this, they appealed to the Latin Fathers and "even to St. Cyril of Alexandria's *Commentary on the Gospel of John.*" Maximus, however, does his best to interpret the Latin doctrine of *Filioque* along Greek patristic lines, claiming that the Latins were "far from making the Son the cause of the Spirit, for they recognize the Father as the one cause of the Son and of the Spirit; the former by generation, the latter by procession." Maximus then states that the Latin *Filioque* was an attempt "to express the Spirit's going forth through the Son"[32] and thus to establish the oneness and inseparable unity of their substance.[33] Maximus also states that he admonished the Romans to be more careful in the usage and meaning of their expressions, adding that he thought the reaction from Constantinople would cause the Romans to be more cautious in the future. This encounter between Rome and the Byzantine East on the question of the procession of the Holy Spirit is the last one hears of such a controversy until the Carolingian period. But already a growing cultural estrangement between the Byzantine East and the Latin West is taking place, an estrangement which will complicate the theological issues involved in the Byzantine-Carolingian Triadological controversy.

---

of 649 as the "sixth" council. Régnon seems correct, however, when he states: "Un document, dont les deux partis contraires peuvent se prévaloir, n'a pu être fabriqué séparément ni par les Grecs ni par les Latins." Théodore de Régnon, *Études de Théologie positive sur La Sainte Trinité* (3 vols.; Paris, 1892-1898), III, 188.

[32]"Τὸ δι' Αὐτοῦ [τοῦ Υἱοῦ] προϊέναι." Although the technical word "procession" is not used here by Maximus, it is clear that this expression is equivalent to the Greek patristic doctrine of the procession of the Spirit through the Son.

[33]*PG* 91, 136.

Cultural Estrangement

An extremely important indicator of the cultural separation of the Byzantine East and the Latin West is that each lacked a knowledge of the other's language. Although there were always those in the papal court who knew Greek, the situation was quite different in the rest of the Latin West.

"There was a time when some scholars were taken in by the claims made of Carolingian authors having a knowledge of Greek; closer examination has shown that any such illusions are naive in the extreme."[34] With the exception of John Scotus Eriugena, none of the Carolingian theologians knew Greek competently. Concerning the "knowledge of Greek" among the Carolingians, Laistner writes:

> If by that phrase is meant the ability correctly to understand a Greek author, theological or secular, or the Greek Bible, then assuredly competent Hellenists of the Carolingian epoch can be counted on one hand. If, on the other hand, it merely implies acquaintance with the Greek alphabet, with a few passages from the Greek liturgy, or with a certain number of isolated Greek words or phrases, generally from the Old and New Testament, then the sum of the accomplished will be somewhat larger, though still small in proportion to the total number of literate men. It has been a radical fault of many modern treatments of the subject that no distinction has been drawn between the first and second class...[35]

Some scholars still attempt to make an exception for Alcuin, claiming that he did in fact know Greek. Such, however, was not the case, and those scholars most familiar with the

---

[34]Philippe Wolff, *The Awakening of Europe*, trans. from the French by Anne Carter (Baltimore: Penguin Books, 1968), p. 95.

[35]M. L. W. Laistner, *Thought and Letters in Western Europe: 500-900* (London, 1931), pp. 191-192.

subject readily admit that Alcuin's use of Greek was "taken over bodily from his predecessors."[36]

> Of the Greek Fathers . . . he knows nothing, except through Latin versions, and of these he makes no considerable use . . . His literary sources are all Latin, nor is there any Greek to be found in what he wrote, apart from some citations copied from Jerome and occasional Greek words from elsewhere.[37]

Although the Carolingian theologians did not know Greek, they at least had the sincere desire to learn the language. The attitude of the Byzantine East toward Latin was, on the other hand, one of indifference and at times contempt. Because of the Greek attitude of "superiority" they not only had no interest in the Latin language but also made no serious attempt to have the works of the Latin Fathers translated into Greek. This attitude of self-sufficiency revealed a lack of a sense of "ecumenicity" and for this the Greek East bears some responsibility for the later estrangement and then schism between the Latin West and the Byzantine East.

The paucity of Latin works translated into Greek is truly remarkable.[38] It is ironic that the Greek Church historians of the fifth and sixth centuries not once mention the name of Augustine. Until the Carolingian controversy with Byzantium, Augustine was known in the Greek East

---

[36]Laistner, p. 192. See also Albert Hauck, *Kirchengeschichte Deutschlands* (3 vols.: Leipzig, 1900), II, 134 and G. J. B. Gaskoin, *Alcuin: His Life and His Work* (New York: Russell & Russell, 1966 reprint; originally published in 1904), p. 54.

[37]A. F. West, *Alcuin and the Rise of the Christian Schools* (New York: Greenwood Press, 1969 reprint; originally published in 1892), p. 91.

[38]The Latin works translated into Greek were Tertullian's *Apologeticum,* some of Cyprian's Letters, the *Acta Martyrum Scillitanorum,* Jerome's *De viris illustribus,* extracts from the works of John Cassian, and Gregory the Great's *Regula Pastoralis.*

only through florilegia[39] translated from the original Latin. Thus the existence of certain Augustinian texts in these florilegia in no way implies that the Greek East had first hand knowledge of the works from which these texts were extracted. And, indeed, extracts from the works of Augustine in these florilegia are not abundant. Of the approximately two-hundred and twenty-eight lines from various works and letters of Augustine appearing in the Greek translations of Latin florilegia there is only one text from *De Trinitate*.[40]

It was only through the Carolingian-Byzantine Triadological controversy that the Byzantine East was presented with numerous lengthy quotations from Augustine's *De Trinitate*. Until that time the triadological thought of Augustine, so well known in the Latin West, remained a closed realm for the Byzantine East.[41]

---

[39]There is a possibility that Augustine's *De gestis Pelagii* was translated into Greek. Altaner's conclusion is most noteworthy: "Damit haben meine Untersuchungen den Beweis erbracht und es offenkundig gemacht, wie erschreckend gross die geistige Abschliessung des sprachverschiedenen Ostens vom lateinischen Westen gewesen ist. Kein griechischer Theologe oder Hierarch hatte in der Zeit vom fünften bis zum neunten Jahrhundert eine auch nur den bescheidensten Ansprüchen genügende Kenntnis von den Schriften und der Theologie des grossen Augustinus. Wenn irgendwo im Schrifttum der griechischen Kirche der Name des grössten abendländischen Theologen erwähnt wird oder ein Zitat aus seinen Schriften uns begegnet, so hat diese Erwähnung in keinem Fall etwas mit einem ernst zu nehmenden Studium der Werke des Bischofs zu tun." Berthold Altaner, "Augustinus in der griechischen Kirche bis auf Photius," *Historisches Jahrbuch,* 71 (1951), 76.

[40]*De Trinitate* II, 9, 6. See Altaner, "Augustinus in der griechischen Kirche bis auf Photius," *Historisches Jahrbuch,* 71 (1951), 62.

[41]Altaner's final conclusion is most accurate: "Abschliessend muss festgestellt werden, dass das Lebenswerk Augustins für die griechische Kirche ein siebenmal versiegeltes Buch war. Daran wird, des bin ich gewiss, nichts geändert werden, auch wenn die weitere Forschung, wie ich hoffe, neue Augustinustexte in griechischen Schriften ausfindig machen wird." Altaner, "Augustinus in der griechischen Kirche bis auf Photius," *Historisches Jahrbuch,* 71 (1951), 76.

Political Estrangement

Byzantine Iconoclasm (726-787 and 813-843), initiated by Emperor Leo III (717-741), contributed greatly to the political and ecclesiastical separation of the Byzantine East and the Latin West. Iconoclasm not only established the background out of which the Triadological controversy emerged but the controversy itself actually began in connection with discussions between the Byzantines and the Franks on the very issue of Iconoclasm.

When Pope Gregory II (715-731) received the imperial edict against icons, he convoked a Roman council which condemned the edict.[42] When in 726/727 the imperial edict was proclaimed in Italy, Pope Gregory II, already suspect in the eyes of the emperor for having withheld a special imperial tax, received an imperial warning against interfering with the imperial policy. Disregarding the imperial warning, Pope Gregory II urged Christians everywhere to resist the heretical edicts of Emperor Leo. Thus a schism began between the Roman See and the See of Constantinople which was to last sixty-one years, from 726 until 787.[43]

Emperor Leo III attempted to take direct action to stop the recalcitrant Pope. Through the Exarchate of Ravenna unsuccessful attempts were made on the life of the Pope. The situation worsened under Pope Gregory III (731-741), who at once sent envoys to Constantinople to protest the imperial policy of Iconoclasm. The papal envoys, however, were prevented from reaching Constantinople; they were stopped, robbed of their letters, and sent back to Italy. When Pope Gregory III held a Roman council which again

---

[42]Mansi 12, 267.

[43]From the establishment of the See of Constantinople until the Seventh Ecumenical Council in 787 there were a total of two-hundred and three years of schism between the Roman and Constantinopolitan Sees. See S. Herbert Scott, *The Eastern Churches and the Papacy* (London, 1928), p. 316.

condemned Iconoclasm, Emperor Leo III despatched a fleet to Italy which, however, was shipwrecked in the Adriatic.

It was at this time and within this hostile atmosphere that Emperor Leo III seized the patrimonies of the Roman See in Calabria and Sicily and, and most importantly, transferred Illyricum from Roman jurisdiction to the jurisdiction of the Patriarch of Constantinople.

Emperor Leo's decisive action with Illyricum is of the greatest significance for the framework in which the Triadological controversy occurs, especially during the second phase of the controversy in the time of Photius. The recovery of the ecclesiastical jurisdiction of Illyricum becomes one of the main objectives of papal policy.

While the Roman See lost the jurisdictional control of Illyricum, the Byzantines suffered the loss of their important foothold in Italy. The Exarchate of Ravenna, a political structure originally organized by Emperor Maurice (582-602), fell to the Lombards in 751. That Emperor Constantine "Copronymus" V (741-775), the successor of Emperor Leo III, "lifted not a finger to save it"[44] is not quite accurate. Emperor Constantine V, busy consolidating his position internally,[45] did in fact attempt to regain the Exarchate of Ravenna by diplomacy, a fact often overlooked. Even the rather accurate statement by the cautious scholar Ostrogorsky leaves no room for Constantine's diplomatic activity:

> No ruler in Byzantium had ever shown so little concern for the maintenance of imperial authority in Italy. While Constantine V was celebrating his victories in the East, Byzantine control in Italy, and with it the conception of a universal Roman Empire, was completely undermined.[46]

---

[44]Romilly Jenkins, *Byzantium: The Imperial Centuries* (New York: Random House, 1969), p. 70.

[45]A revolt by Constantine's elder brother-in-law and a disastrous outbreak of the bubonic plague had rendered Byzantium internally weak.

[46]George Ostrogorsky, *History of the Byzantine State,* trans. from the German by Joan Hussey (New Brunswick: Rutgers University Press, 1957), p. 151.

The imperial envoy John was sent to negotiate with the Lombard Aistulf for the restoration of the Exarchate of Ravenna. But this mission was insurmountably difficult, for the Byzantines had no real bargaining power with which to negotiate.

In Constantinople the Emperor was both developing a rather sophisticated theology of Iconoclasm and preparing for an Ecumenical Council which would sanction his theology and policy. Even in such a situation the Pope seemed to prefer at this time the heretical Emperor to the barbaric Lombards. Pope Stephen (752-757) II (III) wrote imploringly to the Emperor for military aid against the advancing Lombards, who were now moving closer and closer to Rome itself.

The imperial envoy John had returned from Constantinople with the instructions that, although no Byzantine military help could be expected, the Pope was to negotiate personally with Aistulf for the return of the Exarchate.

Realizing in advance that there was little chance of military assistance from Byzantium, and that if it did come it would bring with it an enforcement of Iconoclasm, Pope Stephen II (III) had also written to King Pippin (752-768) of the Franks for aid.[47]

In the spring of 753 the Frankish Duke Autchar and the Frankish Abbot Droctegang arrived in Rome to assure the Pope that Pippin would do everything in his power to help the Roman See. In October of 753 the Pope, accom-

---

[47] The papal letters to Pippin are most interesting, for the Pope wrote in the name of St. Peter and assured Pippin of forgiveness of sins if he helped the Roman See. "I, Peter the Apostle, have been set by the power of Christ to be a light to the whole world... to this apostolic Roman Church of God, entrusted to me, your hope of future reward is attached.... I call on you to defend this Roman state from the hands of its enemies... Our Lady also and all the saints exhort you to have compassion on this city . . . that I may be able to help you at the day of judgment . . . If you come quickly to my aid, then, helped by my prayers, you will... enjoy the gifts of eternal life; but if, as I trust you will not, you delay, know that you are cut off from eternal life." Quoted from volume I, part II of *The Lives of the Popes* by Horace K. Mann (London, 1925), p. 309.

panied by the Frankish escort and the Byzantine envoys, set out for his epochal trip to the Frankish kingdom. Outside of Pavia the papal party was met by representatives of the Lombard Aistulf. Pope Stephen did in fact fulfill the imperial order and asked the Lombards to return the Exarchate of Ravenna.

> In this affair Stephen was acting in the interests of the empire and as a subject of the emperor, under whose commands he had gone to Pavia. But, however great may have been his zeal for the Exarchy, there can be no doubt that his keenest sympathies were centred in the duchy of Rome. This fact is beyond question . . . At Pavia the Pope was playing two roles. The one, which was perfunctory and lacking in confidence, was that of the imperial representative, demanding the restitution of Ravenna. The other, whole-hearted and sanguine, was that of the Roman Pontiff, whose desire was to secure the independence of his fellow-citizens with regard to the Lombards, and his own independence with regard to his fellow-citizens.[48]

The Lombards refused to return the Exarchate of Ravenna to the Byzantines and Pope Stephen continued his journey to the Franks, the results of which were epochal. A new alliance between the Franks and the Papacy emerged, ultimately resulting in the re-creation of the Western Roman Empire with the coronation of Charlemagne in 800. After defeating the Lombards, Pippin returned the Exarchate of Ravenna not to the Byzantine Emperor but to the Pope of Rome.

With this "donation of Pippin" the Papacy would take "refuge in the extraordinary claims of the *Constitutum Constantini,* the Donation of Constantine, that celebrated forgery which can now be attributed—at least in its final and definitive form, to the fertile genius of Pope Leo III and to the year AD 804."[49] Thus the Byzantines had now

---

[48]Louis Duchesne, *The Beginnings of the Temporal Sovereignty of the Popes: 754-1073,* trans. from the French by A. H. Mathew (London, 1907), p. 34.

[49]Jenkins, *op. cit.,* p. 106. Jenkins' conclusion is doubtful.

to contend with the *de facto* breakdown of their concept of One Roman Empire and with, according to their view of the Papacy and the Pentarchy, a new form of papal power which was to exhibit itself quite forcefully in the second phase of the Carolingian-Byzantine Triadological controversy through the person of Pope Nicholas I (858-867).

Byzantium now initiated increased diplomatic activity with the Franks.[50] The two main objectives of Byzantine diplomacy with the Franks were the return of the Exarchate of Ravenna and the hope of winning Pippin to Iconoclasm. Pope Paul I (757-767) was greatly distressed with these Byzantine diplomatic activities and sent several letters to Pippin warning him against the enemies of the faith. Pope Paul I informed Pippin of the Roman position on the veneration of icons and exhorted him to remain faithful to the position of the Roman See.

The Council of Gentilly

The increased Byzantine diplomatic activity with the Franks resulted in the Council of Gentilly (767) which met under the supervision of King Pippin. Although the acts of this council are not extant, information concerning what took place comes from three sources.[51] The council discussed

---

[50]The Byzantines had some contact with the Franks previously. In 508 Clovis accepted from Emperor Anastasius (491-518) the title of consul and the rank of *patricius Romanorum*. In 585 Emperor Maurice supported Gondowald in the recovery of Francia and between 584 and 590 he asked Childebert to take action against the Lombards. And, Pope Stephen granted Pippin the title *patricius Romanorum* with the consent of Emperor Constantine V. "It is true that for the century and a half which elapsed between the last known contact of Heraclius with King Dagobert and the conferment of the Roman patriciate on Pippin, evidence of east-west contact is lacking; but this does not prove that such contact ceased..." Jenkins, *op. cit.*, p. 109.

[51]Einhard (*PL* 104, 386); Ado of Vienne (*PL* 123, 125); and Abbot Regino (*PL* 132, 51).

both the subject of Iconoclasm and the question of the procession of the Holy Spirit.[52] Although some scholars think Roman theologians were present,[53] no reliable evidence on this matter exists.

An interesting question concerning this prelude to the Byzantine-Carolingian Triadological controversy is which side raised the issue of the procession of the Holy Spirit? The opinion that the Greeks were the ones who brought up the subject in order to take attention away from their Iconoclasm is open to criticism. Régnon, admitting that the Byzantine envoys were probably commissioned to bring up the subject of Iconoclasm in an attempt to separate the Franks from the Papacy, does not think that the Byzantines raised the issue of the procession of the Holy Spirit.

> But why raise a question which the Orient did not speak about at all then, and which was of a nature of irritating that which they hoped to gain? It is not at all admissible that a Greek would commit such a political mistake. I think therefore that the Latins

---

[52]Mansi 12, 677: "... quaestio ventilata inter Graecos et Romanos de Trinitate et utrum Spiritus Sanctus, sicut procedit a Patre, ita procedat a Filio." The *Filioque* may have entered the domains of the Franks as early as their conversion to Christianity under King Clovis in 496. In any case, a century later Gregory of Tours, in the introduction to his *History of the Franks*, stated as a part of his profession of faith: "I believe the Holy Spirit to proceed from the Father and the Son." (*Historica Francorum; PL* 71, 161). In Frankish lands the Ecumenical Creed had not yet been interpolated.

[53]Duchesne concludes from the statement "inter Romanos et Graecos" that Romans were present (Duchesne, *op. cit.,* p. 59). Amann thinks that Duchesne has stretched the evidence: "Duchesne a souligné que des 'Romains' étaient présents à cette réunion; peut-être a-t-il attaché trop d' importance au mot lui-même, l'expression 'entre Romains et Grecs' pouvant n'être que la traduction des mots: 'entre les deux Églises orientale et occidentale'." (Émile Amann, *L' époque carolingienne,* volume 6 of *Histoire de l'Église,* ed. by A. Fliche and V. Martin (24 vols.; Paris, 1941), p. 25). It is also indeed curious that Duchesne could write that "the mention of the Trinity is strange. From that time there seems to have been no difference of opinion between East and West on the subject of the Holy Spirit." (Duchesne, *op. cit.,* p. 59).

are the ones who raised the question, and that they wanted to attract the Orientals to the Occidental doctrine.[54]

Hergenröther's conclusions seem accurate. All that is certain is that Byzantine envoys were present, that the theological issues of the veneration of icons and the procession of the Holy Spirit were discussed, and that Pope Paul was satisfied with the results of the council.[55] What is absolutely clear is that the Byzantine East and the Frankish West were divided on the issue of the procession of the Holy Spirit. The Council of Gentilly was an ominous prelude to the Byzantine-Carolingian Triadological controversy. "It is in the assembly of Gentilly that the first spark of a fire was kindled which was destined not to be extinguished despite the efforts of the Church because the flame was always stirred up by the winds of politics."[56]

The preparation for the Byzantine-Carolingian Triadological controversy was now complete. The Latin West had committed itself to the doctrine of the *Filioque,* a part of the Latin West had already interpolated the Ecumenical Creed, and many Latin theologians had assimilated the Augustinian system of triadology. The Greek East, knowing nothing of Augustinian triadology, had remained loyal to the Greek patristic approach to triadology, to the doctrine of the procession of the Spirit from the Father through the Son, and to the Ecumenical decrees concerning the unchangeable nature of the Nicene-Constantinopolitan Creed. The Latin West and the Byzantine East had become culturally, politically, and ecclesiastically estranged. The Roman See had lost Illyricum and Byzantium had lost the Exarchate of Ravenna and with it the *de facto* disintegration of the Byzantine concept of One Universal Roman Empire began.

---

[54]Régnon, *op. cit.,* III, 205.

[55]Josef Hergenröther, *Photius, Patriarch von Konstantinopel: Sein Leben, Seine Schriften und Das Griechische Schisma* (3 vols.; Regensburg, 1867; reprinted in 1966, Darmstadt), I, 693.

[56]Régnon, *op. cit.,* p. 205.

And the Roman Pope had emerged with powers which, according to the Byzantines, were incompatible with the Byzantine interpretation of Papacy and the Pentarchy. It was now only a matter of time before the Triadological controversy would erupt within this atmosphere. The initial attack came not from the Byzantine East but from the Carolingian West.

CHAPTER III

The *Libri Carolini*

The first Carolingian effort not only to propagate the *Filioque* doctrine but also to oppose it to the Eastern doctrine of the procession of the Holy Spirit from the Father through the Son presents itself quite caustically in the monumental *Libri Carolini,* a work appropriately referred to as a "thoroughly unique summa of Carolingian-Christian thought and knowledge."[1] The *Libri Carolini* were written expressly to challenge the acts of the Seventh Ecumenical Council (787).[2] Responding to the acts of the Seventh Ecumenical

---

[1] Wolfram von den Steinen, "Entstehungsgeschichte der *Libri Carolini,*" *Quellen und Forschungen aus italienischen Archiven und Bibliotheken,* XXI (1929-30), 76.

[2] Charlemagne may have had personal as well as theological and political motives for initiating the *Libri Carolini*. His daughter Rotrude "had been engaged to Constantine, the Emperor of the Greeks" [Einhard, *The Life of Charlemagne,* trans. by Lewis Thorpe (Baltimore: Penguin Books, 1969), p. 74] in 781. It may well have been Empress Irene who broke off the marriage plans between her son Constantine VI (780-797) and Rotrude, an act which might have infuriated Charlemagne. After peace had been established with the See of Rome at the Seventh Ecumenical

45

Council which Pope Hadrian I (772-795) sent him,³ Charlemagne charged his theologians to prepare a list of objections, known as the *capitulare,* which were then brought to Rome by Angilbert, the son-in-law of Charlemagne.⁴

That the *capitulare* were not the *Libri Carolini* but rather a list of objections to the acts of the Seventh Ecumenical Council is obvious from an analysis of the lengthy response of Pope Hadrian I.⁵ The papal response explicitly states that the first objection of the *capitulare* concerned itself with an attack against the expression that the Spirit proceeds from the Father through the Son.⁶ The papal response then quotes the *"reprehensio"* from the Carolingian *capitulare.*

> *That* Tarasius is not correct in professing that the Holy Spirit proceeds not from the Father and the Son, according to the faith of the Nicene Creed, but that he proceeds from the Father through the Son.⁷

It is noteworthy that this *"reprehensio"* from the first

Council, "the Frankish alliance seemed less necessary to Irene; it is said that she feared chiefly lest the mighty Charles should become too strong a support to his son-in-law and help him be master of the Empire." [Charles Diehl, *Byzantine Empresses,* trans. from the French by Harold Bell and Theresa de Kerpely (London, 1964), p. 80]. This, along with Charlemagne's anger at not having been informed of the plans for the coming council to which none of his Frankish theologians were invited, may well account for his personal reasons for sponsoring the *Libri Carolini.* In addition to the personal and political reasons, there were also theological factors, the chief of which was Charlemagne's semi-Iconoclasm.

³The fact that the Latin translation of the acts of the Council sent to Charlemagne was poor has no bearing on the problem of the *Filioque* but rather with the interpretation of iconodulism as defined by the Council.

⁴Mansi 13, 759.

⁵Pope Hadrian's lengthy response [*Epistola Hadriani Papae ad Carolum Regem;* Mansi 13, 759-810] reveals that the Papacy considered the Carolingian attack on an Ecumenical Council quite serious and a direct challenge to the "catholicity" of the Church.

⁶Mansi 13, 760.

⁷Mansi 13, 760. Tarasius was Patriarch Tarasius of the See of Constantinople (784-806).

objection of the *capitulare* becomes the title of the third chapter of the third book in the *Libri Carolini* with only two slight changes, the first of which is most significant. Instead of stating *"that* Tarasius is not correct," the *Libri Carolini* worded its chapter title *"whether* Tarasius is correct..."[8] This indicates that the author of the *Libri Carolini* is obviously accepting the challenge of the papal *"responsio"* in order to disprove it. What then was the *"responsio"* of Pope Hadrian I concerning this issue?

In his *"responsio"* to the Carolingian *"reprehensio"* Pope Hadrian writes that "Tarasius has not pronounced this dogma by himself but he has confessed it by the doctrine of the Holy Fathers."[9] Pope Hadrian states that this doctrine is in perfect accord with the teaching of the Roman See.[10] He then stresses that this doctrine was taught by both the Latin and the Greek Fathers, quoting brief selections from Athanasius, Gregory of Nyssa, Hilary, Basil, Ambrose, Gregory of Nazianzus, Cyril of Alexandria, Pope Leo, Pope Gregory, Sophronius, and Augustine.[11] The papal *"responsio"* concludes with an explicit warning.

> We have already shown that the divine dogmas of this Council are irreprehensible ... For should anyone say he differs from the

---

[8]*Libri Carolini sive Caroli Magni Capitulare de Imaginibus,* ed. by Hubert Bastgen, *Monumenta Germaniae Historica, Legum Sectio III, Concilia Tomi II Supplementum* (Hanover and Leipzig, 1924), Book III, p. 110. (The *Libri Carolini* is hereafter cited as *LC* and the *Monumenta Germaniae Historica* as *MGH*).

[9]Mansi 13, 760: "Hoc dogma Tarasius non per se explanavit, sed per doctrinam sanctorum patrum confessus est." Because of the parallel structure of "per se" and "per doctrinam sanctorum patrum" it is clear that "per se" refers to Tarasius and not to "Hoc dogma."

[10]Mansi 13, 760. Even if Pope Hadrian I had accepted the doctrine of *Filioque,* there would have been no reason for him to reject the *per Filium* because Latin theology considered the *per Filium* as a proof of the *Filioque.* It is the Greek interpretation of *per Filium* which requires a rejection of the *Filioque.*

[11]Pope Hadrian quotes from Augustine's sermons on the Ascension and Pentecost as well as from books 4 and 15 of *De Trinitate.*

> Creed of the above-mentioned Council, he risks differing with the Creed of the Six Holy Councils, since these Fathers spoke not according to their own opinions but according to the holy definitions previously laid down. In the acts of the Sixth Holy Council it is written among other things that "this Creed had been sufficient for the perfect knowledge and confirmation of religion."[12]

Having received the lengthy reply of Pope Hadrian I, Charlemagne commissioned his theologians to write a full reply. It is here assumed that the *Libri Carolini* were composed and corrected between 790 and 791 and that the dominant author was Theodulf of Orléans, not Alcuin.[13] Although the theological problem of the procession of the Holy Spirit is only a peripheral issue in the *Libri Carolini*, it is nevertheless considered a serious problem.

In the third book of the *Libri Carolini* the author states that "at the outset of this work of ours we promised to leave nothing undiscussed or passed over in silence which was found worthy of censure in the synod which concerned itself with the *adoration* of images."[14]

> It is therefore not appropriate that a discussion be omitted from our work concerning the fact that Tarasius teaches in his profession of faith that the Holy Spirit does not proceed from the Father only,—as certain men profess who, although they are silent as to how he proceeds from the Son, yet believe fully that he proceeds from the Father and the Son,—and not from the Father and the Son as the whole universal Church believes and professes, but "from the Father through the Son."[15]

The author of the *Libri Carolini* is convinced that the profession of the Spirit's procession from the Father through the Son could cause a "pernicious poison" to arise."[16]

---

[12]Mansi 13, 764-766; *PL* 98, 1272.

[13]See the research by Ann Freeman, "Theodulf of Orléans and the *Libri Carolini,*" *Speculum,* XXXII (1957), 663-705; and "Further Studies in the *Libri Carolini,*" *Speculum,* XL (1965), 203-289 and *Speculum,* XLVI (1971), 597-612.

[14]*LC*, 110.

[15]*LC*, 110.

[16]*Ibid.*

The first objection of the author of the Libri *Carolini* is that the expression "through the Son" is imprecise. "If definition in other fields should be so clear and enlightening ...much more should a definition of faith be clear and understandable without any ambiguity or intricacy."[17]

The second objection, which is of course based on the assumption that "it is rightly and customarily believed that the Holy Spirit proceeds from the Father and the Son,"[18] is that if the Spirit proceeds "through the Son," then the Spirit could be considered a creature. The reasoning, shaped as a result of the Arian and Adoptionist heresies in Spain, is based on the text from the Gospel of John which states that "all things were made through [*per*] him."[19] It is explicitly stated in the *Libri Carolini* that the reason the Spirit proceeds from the Father and the Son is that "it is believed that he does not proceed through the Son like a creature which was made through him."[20] A strange analogy is then attempted. Stating that the "preposition *from* [*ex*] has one force [*and*]the preposition *through* [*per*] another force,"[21] the author of the *Libri Carolini* then attempts to proof his trinitarian position by demonstrating that since the Son of God was born from man and not through man, therefore "it can be asked whether the Holy Spirit can rightly be said to proceed from the Father *through* the Son."[22] The fear of the author is the "poisonous cup" of Arianism, for "Arius maintained blasphemously that the Holy Spirit is a creature and was created through the Son just as the rest of creation."[23] The author then demonstrates through various Biblical texts that the Spirit is not a creature, but

---

[17]*Ibid.*
[18]*Ibid.*
[19]John 1:3; "δι' αὐτοῦ" in Greek, "per ipsum" in Latin.
[20]*LC*, 110.
[21]*Ibid.*
[22]*LC*, 110-111.
[23]*LC*, 111.

divine. Hence, according to the logics of the analogy, he cannot proceed *through* the Son because the Spirit would then be a creature. The author's theological reasoning at this point is, however, rooted in a naive Biblicism and in a rather poor metaphysical understanding of creation and procession. The author of the *Libri Carolini* had falsely thought he detected an Arian tendency in the *per Filium*.

The third objection is indeed noteworthy. The author of the *Libri Carolini,* defending so ardently the *Filioque* which he obviously thought was in the original Creed, actually uses the same charge against the Greek East which the Greek East will later bring against the Latin West. He objects to the *per Filium* because it was not in the original Creed, because it was not "authorized."

> While [the Holy Spirit] is proved to be God and Creator by this testimony and while the whole Catholic Church believes he proceeds from the Father and the Son, it ought to be asked whether it is necessary to profess that he proceeds from the Father through the Son and not rather from the Father and the Son, since a profession of this sort is not found to have been made by the Holy Fathers either in the Nicene Creed or that of Chalcedon... It is not customary for the Synodical Creed to profess that he proceeds from the Father through the Son because in order to proceed from the Father, the Holy Spirit does not need the help of another to proceed from another.[24]

Indeed, this last statement is most interesting, especially in the light of the later Photian reaction to Latin triadology. One of Photius' main points is that either the procession of the Spirit from the Father is perfect or there is no perfection in God the Father, which is contrary to Christian teaching. If then the procession of the Spirit from the Father is perfect, why is there a procession from the Son also? The author of the *Libri Carolini* is not aware of the theological implications of his own statement concerning his own doctrine.

The fourth objection to the statement that the Spirit

---

[24]*LC,* 112.

The Libri Carolini

proceeds from the Father through the Son comes directly from Augustine. Since the Spirit is the Spirit of the Son, he must therefore proceed from the Son.

> He is called the Spirit of the Son as Paul testifies: "Anyone who does not have the Spirit of Christ does not belong to him." (Rom. 8:9). And therefore he is called the Spirit of both because he is proved to be of one substance and nature, proceeding from the Father and the Son. If he were called unbegotten, two Fathers would be professed; if begotten, two sons would be professed. But because he is neither Father nor Son, he is therefore said to be neither unbegotten nor begotten, but proceeding from both.[25]

He then quotes directly from Augustine's *De Trinitate:* "But he would be called the Son of the Father and of the Son, if—a thing abhorrent to all the faithful—they had both begotten him. Therefore the Spirit has not been begotten by both of them, but he proceeds from both."[26] He continues to use Augustinian material to prove that the Spirit proceeds from the Father and the Son, especially Augustine's emphasis on Christ's breathing the Spirit on the disciples. "Unless he proceeded from him, in vain would he have given (the Holy Spirit) to his disciples by breathing on them."[27]

And, finally, the author of the *Libri Carolini* appeals to mystery, for the inner life of the Trinity escapes man's comprehension.

> If anyone asks how . . . the Holy Spirit proceeds from the Father and the Son and yet is not preceded by those from whom he proceeds, let him know that these and similar matters are inscrutable and incomprehensible to our frail human understanding. Who would consider these things? Who would understand them? If we do not comprehend the secrets of Christ's human nativity, how will we understand the mysteries of the Divine nature?[28]

Admitting that "it is indeed difficult to distinguish

---

[25]*LC*, 112.
[26]*Ibid.*; *De Trinitate* XV, 26, 47.
[27]*LC*, 113.
[28]*Ibid.*

generation from procession in that co-eternal, incorporeal, ineffable, unchangeable and inseparable Trinity,"[29] the author of the *Libri Carolini* then states that it suffices "to believe this, to hold it firmly, to confess it with our whole heart: the unbegotten Father, the begotten Son, the Holy Spirit neither created nor born but proceeding from the Father and the Son."[30] There is, however, one most noteworthy stipulation made by the author of the *Libri Carolini*. The stipulation is that "in the confession of the Faith all whims, *all verbal novelties be avoided* and in these words and these statements the confession of the faithful be strengthened, matters which the Holy and Ecumenical Synods have treated in the Creed."[31]

It is quite clear that the author of the *Libri Carolini* believed that the Filioque was in the original Creed. It is also clear that when he refers to the confession of the faith which all the faithful must "hold firmly," he is referring to the Athanasian Creed. As a result not of bad will but of historical ignorance the author of the *Libri Carolini* advances the *Filioque* in a quite theologically unsophisticated manner. His appeal to Augustine, and also to Isidore of Seville, is historically valid. But his appeal to the Ecumenical Councils is simply historically inaccurate. His reference to Isidore of Seville and his complete certainty that the *Filioque* was a part of the original Creed seem to indicate the Spanish origin of the author.

It appears that at the Council of Frankfurt (794), whose acts are not extant,[32] the *Libri Carolini* were presented and

---

[29]*Ibid.*

[30]*Ibid.*

[31]*LC*, 113.

[32]See Gert Haendler, *Epochen Karolingischer Theologie* (Berlin, 1958), p. 36. Amann writes: "Les documents qui permettent de s'en faire une idée sont de deux sortes: (1) Les narrations des Chroniques ou des historiens contemporains. Toutes les Annales en parlent, à l'année 794; récit très complet et très circonstancié dans la Chronique de Moissac; c'est ce récit que nous prenons comme cadre, en y ajoutant les précisions transmises par

approved. The main objective of this council, which was considered "universal" by the Carolingians,[33] was to combat the heresy of Adoptianism in Spain. This council issued fifty-six "capitula," the thirty-third of which stated that "one is to teach to all the faithful the Catholic Faith in the Trinity, the Our Father, and the Creed." There seems to be little doubt that the "Catholic Faith in the Trinity" referred to the Athanasian Creed.[34] Three of the four letters attached to the canons of the Council of Frankfurt teach the procession of the Spirit from the Father and the Son.[35]

---

ailleurs; (2) Le dossier envoyé aux Espagnols à l'issue du concile et qui comprend: 1) la lettre d'Hadrien; 2) le *Libellus sacrosyllabus episcoporum Italiae;* 3) l'*Epistola episcoporum Franciae;* 4) l'*Epistola Caroli magni ad Elipandum.* Ces quatre pièces qui forment bloc ont été copiées ensemble de fort bonne heure. Elles se lisent à la suite dans un manuscrit copié en 821 pour Baturic, évêque de Ratisbonne." Amann, *L'Époque carolingienne, op. cit.,* p. 142.

[33]Hefele-Leclercq, *Histoire des Conciles* (Paris, 1910), III, part II, p. 1046: "... le célèbre concile de Francfort, dont parlent presque tous les chroniqueurs de cette époque, et qu'ils appellent souvent *universalis.*"

[34]*Ibid.,* p. 1059.

[35]Pope Hadrian's letter (Mansi 13, 871); Paulinus' letter (Mansi 13, 878), and Charlemagne's letter (Mansi 13, 905-906).

CHAPTER IV

Paulinus of Aquileia and Alcuin

The Council of Friuli

The Carolingian "capitulare," the response of Pope Hadrian I, the *Libri Carolini* and their probable dogmatization at the Council of Frankfurt in 794 set the Carolingian West not only against the Byzantine East but also against the See of Rome.

Paulinus, made Patriarch of Aquileia by Charlemagne,[1] was commissioned by the Council of Frankfurt to present a patristic refutation to the Adoptianism of the Spaniards Felix and Elipandus. However, the council actually convoked by Paulinus in 796 or 797 concerned itself primarily with the problem of the Creed and the addition of the *Filioque* to it. It may be that Paulinus was also charged to treat this subject. At any event, it can be rightly concluded that Paulinus

---

[1] See Carl Giannoni, *Paulinus II, Patriarch von Aquileia: Ein Beitrag zur Kirchengeschichte Österreichs im Zeitalter Karls des Grossen* (Wien, 1896).

considered the addition of the *Filioque* to the Creed of greatest importance. He was perhaps uneasy with the firm reply of Pope Hadrian I on this issue.

The council convoked by Paulinus, the Council of Friuli, was epochal. In one of the most interesting records[2] of *Filioque* history Paulinus developed a *theology of interpolation* which provided a theological justification for the interpolated *Filioque*.

Paulinus claims that the definition of both the Nicene and the Nicene-Constantinopolitan Creed is "inviolable." After stating that "it was ordained by the Holy Synods that no one be allowed to teach or compose another Creed of faith other than the one they decreed," Paulinus then begins his *theology of interpolation,* stating that "perhaps according to the intention of the Fathers" something which does not contradict either the meaning of the Creed or the intention of the Fathers can be added legitimately to the Ecumenical Creed. What is at issue, he states, "is not adding or subtracting anything from the faith which the Fathers taught ... What is at issue is *craftily adding or subtracting* what is contrary to their sacred intentions."

To support his position Paulinus calls attention to the "addition" to the original Creed by the Council of Constantinople. If the Second Ecumenical Council could "add" something to the original Creed, then the Holy Fathers of the Second Ecumenical Council precisely laid the precedent for future additions. According to Paulinus, the original Ecumenical Creed was "published" by the Holy Fathers as an "aid," as a "measuring device." Hence, when the "thorns of deception" arise, it is the duty of the Church "to seek out from the roots such bushes which grow from an injurious source." All the "little branches of iniquity" must be cut down.

The most efficient way of cutting down heresy is through the Creed. Thus, according to Paulinus, it is not only

---

[2]Mansi 13, 830ff; *PL* 99, 293-296.

legitimate but sometimes necessary to add statements to the Creed, as the Fathers of the Second Ecumenical Council did. However, one can add to the Creed only on two conditions. First, an addition to the Creed is permissible only if it clarifies the Faith in opposition to heresies. Secondly, an addition to the Creed must be in accordance with the *intention* of the Holy Fathers and it must not contradict the original meaning of the Creed. Paulinus also implicitly teaches that an addition should be made by conciliar action, but he fails to distinguish between the authority of an Ecumenical Council and a local council. The *Filioque* addition, according to Paulinus, had conciliar authority and met the two conditions of interpolation.

> But later, on account of those manifest heretics who murmur that the Holy Spirit is only of the Father and proceeds only from the Father, the words "who proceeds from the Father and the Son" were added. Yet these Holy Fathers were not blameworthy, as if they had added or subtracted something from the faith of the 318 Fathers. They did not think *contrary* to the intentions of the Fathers, but rather strove to supplement their pure understanding with a sound usage.

What remains puzzling is Paulinus' reference to the Holy Fathers who added the *Filioque*. It is possible that Paulinus is referring to the Council of Frankfurt, a council considered by the Carolingians to be "universal." The Council of Frankfurt may have sanctioned the interpolated Creed along with the approval of the *Libri Carolini*. If he is not referring to the Council of Frankfurt, he may then be alluding to the earlier Spanish councils. If he is referring to neither, then the historical reference is simply unknown. Also puzzling is his reference to those who "murmur that the Holy Spirit is only of the Father and proceeds only from the Father." This statement implies that there was a controversy on the very subject of the procession of the Holy Spirit. But whether he is referring to a past controversy or a contemporary one is unknown.

Paulinus then declares that "those who added the words 'who proceeds from the Father and the Son' had read this very truth in the Gospel." The next step in his *theology of interpolation* is to prove that the procession of the Holy Spirit from the Father and the Son is Biblical. His basic premise is that the Father and the Son are consubstantial, and that the Holy Spirit is also consubstantial with the Father and the Son. "If, therefore, as He testified (John 14:9, 10), the Father is in the Son and the Son is in the Father inseparably and substantially, how are we to believe that, since the Holy Spirit is consubstantial with the Father and the Son, he does not proceed always from the Father and the Son essentially and inseparably?" Following Augustine's treatment of the Biblical text, Paulinus then claims that since the Son breathed the Holy Spirit on the disciples, the Spirit must proceed from the Son also. Again he returns to the consubstantiality and inseparability of the Divine Persons of the Trinity.

> It has often been defined without any doubt by us and by our predecessors that the works of the Holy Trinity are always inseparable. Thus, it is believed that the Holy Spirit proceeds from the Son, since no one doubts that he proceeds from the Father. But we can better prove this if we consider the acts and deeds of the Apostles.

All the examples then given by Paulinus refer to the temporal mission of the Holy Spirit. After giving examples of the inseparability of the works of the Holy Trinity, Paulinus exclaims:

> How solidly established were the Holy Catholic Fathers in the faith, professing that the Holy Spirit proceeds from the Father! How gloriously established were those also who confessed that he proceeds from the Father and the Son!

Paulinus concludes that the "Holy Spirit is true God. He is truly and properly the Holy Spirit, not born, not created, but proceeding eternally and inseparably from the Father and the Son." This is almost a direct quotation from the Athanasian Creed.

With great solemnity the interpolated Ecumenical Creed is then read, after which Paulinus theologizes on the meaning of the statements in the Creed. In conclusion Paulinus stresses the absolute necessity for everyone to commit the interpolated Creed to memory.

> This very sincere purity of the Catholic Faith, therefore, we wish all priests of God and all ranks of the Church to hold in memory by learning it clearly, with utmost zeal and without any adulteration so that not even one jot be omitted or increased, and to bequeath it to their posterity to be learned . . . If . . . anyone (is) . . . sluggish with weak talent . . . let him memorize it before the anniversary of this venerable council . . . Otherwise, consider that it will be difficult for you to avoid ecclesiastical censure . . . Let every Christian know the Creed . . . by heart— every age, both sexes, every condition: males, females, youths, old men, slaves, freemen, boys, married couples, unwed girls, because without this blessing no one can receive a part in the kingdom of heaven . . .
> My flock, we are not forming new rules or eagerly pursuing empty inventions; but we considered it worthwhile to renew them in a contemporary style, after the sacred pages of the canons of the Fathers had been reviewed and we had embraced with devout reverence those things which endure.

Paulinus, appending a new version of the liturgy which, with few exceptions, is still the present Roman *Latin* Mass, sent copies of the acts of the Council of Friuli to Charlemagne and to Alcuin. Having received his copy, Alcuin wrote enthusiastically to Paulinus: "I have often urged our Lord the King to obtain a clear and intelligible version (*i.e.* of the Creed) on . . . one sheet . . . and have it distributed, propagated, and learned by all . . . now you have done this . . . we must see that it is used."[3]

Thus, by the combined efforts of Paulinus and Alcuin the interpolated Ecumenical Creed received theological justification in the Carolingian West. Either after the Council of Frankfurt or after the Council of Friuli the interpolated Ecumenical Creed began to be sung during the liturgy at the royal chapel in Aachen.

---

[3]*Epistola* 139; *MGH, Epistolae* IV, p. 220.

Alcuin

Alcuin, "constant reader of Augustine,"[4] wrote a work in 802 entitled *De Fide sanctae et individuae Trinitatis,* a work which he himself considered his most important. The work was intended as a "handbook" and, according to the *Vita Alcuini,* the book became most useful. This work has been referred to as "the beginning of Mediaeval Theology"[5] precisely because of its use of the dialectic method, a method which Alcuin readily and often admits he borrowed from Augustine. In a letter to Charlemagne[6] which accompanied this work Alcuin writes:

> I have directed a sermon to your most holy authority concerning the faith of the Holy and Undivided Trinity under the form of a little book fitted to the hand so that praise and faith of the divine wisdom might be proved by the judgment of the most wise of men. Clearly I did not think wisdom more worthy in any way than the gift of your imperial majesty, nor did I think anyone equally worthy in accepting such an excellent gift . . . since some call me by the name teacher (not that I deserve it), I perform my duty that I might convince those who do not think it is useful that your most noble intention is to wish to learn the *dialectic of learning* which our father Augustine thought exceedingly necessary in his books about the Holy Trinity . . . he proved it possible to explain the most profound questions about the Holy Trinity only in the subtlety of categories . . .

What is most significant about the trinitarian section of Alcuin's *De Fide sanctae et individuae Trinitatis*[7] is that it is not only thoroughly Augustinian in meaning but also

---

[4]Eleanor S. Duckett, *Alcuin, Friend of Charlemagne* (New York, 1951), p. 268.

[5]Albert Hauck, *Kirchengeschichte Deutschlands* (3 vols.; Leipzig, 1900), II, 146.

[6]*Epistola Nuncupatoria* (*PL* 101, 11-14).

[7]Book One, 1-15; *PL* 101, 13-22.

simply a condensed repetition of Augustine's *De Trinitate* from which he freely borrowed.

The first aspect of Augustinian triadology which Alcuin has mastered is Augustine's doctrine of relations. "Certain things are said relatively as Father to Son and Son to Father, and as the Holy Spirit relates to the Father and the Son... in truth, that God is Father is said relatively ... Father, Son, and Holy Spirit is said relatively." And "this pattern of relationship ought to be understood in the persons of the Holy Trinity."

The second aspect of Augustinian triadology which Alcuin has assimilated is Augustine's teaching that the Holy Spirit is the bond or communion of the Father and the Son. "The Holy Spirit, who proceeds equally from the Father and the Son is, so to speak, the ineffable communion of the Father and the Son."

The third aspect of Augustinian triadology assimilated by Alcuin is Augustine's teaching that all divine attributes in God are identical to essence. "It is not one thing to be God and another to be great or one thing to be God and another to be good, but it is the same thing for him *to be* and to be great, *to be* and to be good..."

Relatively, each person has its own property. "The Holy Spirit has this property that he proceeds equally from the Father and the Son." Quoting almost directly from Augustine, Alcuin writes that "he does not proceed from the Father into the Son and from the Son to sanctify creation as certain people who understood badly thought should be believed, but he proceeds from both at once because the Father begot such a Son so that in whatever manner the Holy Spirit proceeds from one, he also proceeds from the other."

Alcuin, according to the evidence from the *Epistola Nuncupatoria*, believes firmly that what he has written comes from the authority of the "works in the Catholic Faith." But what is more important for Alcuin even than the "weight" of the "authority" of Augustine is the imperial sanction. "Therefore," he writes to Charlemagne, "if the right hand of your dignity is extended to the reading, no one will be able rightly to spurn my words because the authority of your approval will count more than the devotion of my writing." If the work does receive the *imperial* sanction, then "it should be impressed . . . in the hearts of all."

In his *Commentary on the Gospel of John* Alcuin reveals his rather unsophisticated assimilation of Augustinian triadology. He has so thoroughly assimilated Augustine's theology of the unity, oneness, and absolute simplicity of the Divine Essence that a great confusion concerning the Divine Persons ensues.

> Undoubtedly the Father is rightly called the "first principle," and the Son the "first principle"; yet there are not two first principles. Just as the Father is God and the Son is God, there are yet not two Gods, but one God must be affirmed. So the Father is the first principle, and the Son the first principle, yet there are not two first principles, but one first principle must be confessed. Therefore the Holy Spirit also is the first principle, yet there are not three first principles, Father, Son, and Holy Spirit, but one first principle.[8]

What is clear from this unclear statement is that the personal existence of the Father, Son, and Holy Spirit is relative. The first principle in the Godhead is the Divine Essence. According to the logics of Alcuin the Holy Spirit would necessarily proceed from himself.

Alcuin's work became quite popular and during the second phase of the Triadological controversy with Byzantium the Latin theologians appeal to Alcuin as one of their "authorities."

---

[8] The English translation is from H. Watkin-Jones, *The Holy Spirit in the Mediaeval Church* (London, 1922), p. 43.

CHAPTER V

The Jerusalem Controversy and Its Aftermath

The Letter of the Pilgrim Monks

In 802 Emperor Charlemagne, now the Christian protector of the Holy Land, had sent an ambassador to the Caliph of Bagdad, Harun al-Rashid. Toward the end of 806 this ambassador returned with an envoy of the Caliph and with two monks, Abbot Georg Egilbald and a certain Felix. While in Aachen, the two monks heard the Ecumenical Creed sung with the *Filioque* interpolation and, upon returning to Jerusalem, they introduced the *Filioque* into the Latin text of the Ecumenical Creed in order to conform with "imperial" practices. When the Greek monks at Jerusalem discovered that the Latin monks had added to the Creed, a serious controversy erupted.

The events which took place are vividly described in

a letter which the Latin monks wrote to Pope Leo III (795-816).[1]

The Letter of the Pilgrim Monks Living On Mount Olivet to the Roman Pontiff, Leo III. (Year 807).

The Congregation of Mt. Olivet to our most holy and most reverend lord in Christ and father, Leo, supreme pontiff and universal pope of the holy apostolic see of the city of Rome.

Lord Father, the Lord has deigned to exalt you above all priests, and your holy see is exalted above all Christian sees. To you Christ has deigned to say from his mouth, "Thou art Peter" (Matt. 16:18), etc. Most benign Father, we strangers who are living in the holy city of Jerusalem, love no man on earth more than you, and as much as possible in these holy places, we your servants, prostrate on the ground with tears, pour forth our prayers to the Lord day and night on your behalf. Accordingly, we are informing you of the tribulation which we are suffering here. John, who was from the monastery of St. Sabbas, whom your servant, Iguminus Thedulus knows, is raised above us, saying that the Franks who are on Mt. Olivet are heretics. He also said to us that all you Franks are heretics, and he reproved our faith by saying that it is no better than heresy. And we said to him: "Brother, be silent. Because if you call us heretics, you are calling the holy, apostolic See heretical."

And he disturbed us so much that on the day of the birth of our Lord, in the holy place in holy

---

[1] *Epistola Peregrinorum Monachorum in Monte Oliveti Habitantium ad Leonem III Pontificem Romanum* (*PL* 129, 1257-60). Translated by Raymond Ciuba and the author. This text was published by the author in Volume VI of *Transactions of the Association of Russian-American Scholars* (1972), 317-319.

Bethlehem, where our Lord the Redeemer of the human race deigned to be born for the salvation of the world, he sent laymen who wanted to throw us out, saying "You are heretics and the books which you have are heretical." But through your holy prayers and faith the Lord strengthened us. And they were not able to throw us out. We all said: "Here we wish to die, for you will not be able to throw us out." Then all we, your servants, raised our voices and said even to the priests who are in the holy city: "Fathers and brothers, look at this man who says such things and other things against us and against the holy Roman faith, because such things we have never heard about our people."

After this, on the Lord's Day, the priests with other clergy and the people gathered across from the Lord's holy sepulchre, near the holy place of Calvary, and those same priests inquired about our faith concerning the way we say the Creed. We said we believe just as the holy Roman Church does. "We have said and still say in our language what you do not say in Greek. In the *Glory to the Father* you do not say *'as it was in the beginning,'* and in the *Glory to God in the Highest* you do not say, *'Thou alone art most High.'* You recite the *Our Father* differently, and in the Creed we say more than you, *'Who proceeds from the Father and the Son,'* because of which words that John, an enemy of his own soul, says that we are heretics."

We begged the men of Jerusalem saying: "Do not listen to[2] this man, and do not accuse us of heresy. If you say that we are heretics, you impute heresy to the throne of Blessed Peter, and if you say that, you lead yourselves into sin." The priests wrote

---

[2] Alternate readings are *audire* and *odire* (hate), the first of which is obviously preferred.

us a letter about our faith, about what we should believe. They said to us, "Do you believe just as the Church of the Holy Resurrection of the Lord does?" We said that we believe the same as the Holy Resurrection of the Lord and the Holy Apostolic Roman See. Then the archdeacon in St. Constantine's went up to the prominent place with us and read the letter to the people. All of us, your servants, anathematized every heresy and all who accused the Holy Apostolic Roman See of heresy. And now, lord and most benign Father, deign to think about us, your servants, who are your sheep although we are far away. The whole world has been entrusted to you, as your holiness knows, for the Lord said to Peter, "If you love me, Peter, feed my sheep" (Jn. 21:16). Most benign father, while I, your servant Leo, was in your holy presence, and in the devout presence of your son, the most pious Emperor lord Charles, we heard it said in his chapel in the Creed of the faith *"who proceeds from the Father and the Son."* And in the homilies of St. Gregory, which your son the Emperor lord Charles gave us, it says in the sermons for the octave of Easter, "But his sending forth is his procession; he proceeds from the Father and the Son." And in the rule of St. Benedict, which your son lord Charles gave us, and which contains the faith about the Holy and inseparable Trinity, it says, "I believe that the Holy Spirit is true God, proceeding from the Father and the Son." And in the dialogue, which your holiness deigned to give us, it says the same thing.

And so a great confusion has been created among us in the holy city by that same John, since he says that the Holy Spirit does not proceed from the Father and the Son. Thus, he spread a great error through all the monasteries. He demanded our profession of faith and our books, saying that lord Gregory's books must not be accepted. Whence, holy Father, again and again we ask and beseech you, prostrate on the ground with tears, through the Father, Son, and Holy Spirit, which is called one inseparable Trinity, that you deign to search out both in Greek as well as in Latin the holy Fathers who composed the Creed concerning that phrase where it is said: *"Who proceeds from the Father and the Son."* In Greek they do not say as we do, but rather they say: *"Who proceeds from the Father,"* and they view that phrase which we say in Latin as a serious matter. Deign to give an order to your son the Emperor lord Charles because we heard the words *"Who proceeds from the Father and the Son"* in his chapel. Deign to inform us, your servants here, since no form of this mystery seems as pleasant to us as your holy countenance and holy prayer and your intercession or remembrance. Whence, most benign Father, we beg of your most holy piety that you would deign to receive favorably the priest John as also these your servants, who, governed by God, have come to the dignity of your office, and direct us, your servants, with a definite order. Dominic, Theodore, Arimund, Gregory, John, Leo and the entire congregation of holy Mt. Olivet commend themselves, your servants, to your sacred prayers which are worthy of God. May the Lord our God, who is said to be blessed unto all ages, deign to rule over and protect you, most holy Father, and all who are with you, and may he guard you in everything, through everything, by his holy mercy, for the exaltation of his holy Church, for the salvation of your soul, and for our joy.

Some noteworthy facts emerge from this controversy. First, there is little doubt that the interpolated Creed had for some years now received "imperial" sanction. Secondly, the Latin monks consider the *Filioque* as only a liturgical difference, no more important than other liturgical differences between the Latins and the Greeks. Thirdly, what has quite perplexed the Latin monks is the *seriousness* with which the Greeks react to the *Filioque*. Fourthly, their claim that the Rule of St. Benedict contained the *Filioque* means that the Carolingians had appended either the interpolated Ecumenical Creed or the Athanasian Creed to the Rule of St. Benedict. And fifthly, it is noteworthy that the bond between the Carolingians and the Papacy is so strong that the monks think an attack on Frankish practices is also an attack on the Roman See.

Pope Leo's Letter to the Eastern Churches

Pope Leo III responded by sending a letter to "all the Churches of the East," a letter which obviously also went to the Latin monks on Mt. Olivet. Pope Leo states at the beginning of the letter that "we are sending you this Creed of the Orthodox Faith so that you and everyone may hold the correct and inviolate faith according to the Holy Roman Catholic and Apostolic Church."[2a] Concerning the procession of the Holy Spirit, Pope Leo professes:

> The Holy Spirit proceeds equally from the Father and the Son and is consubstantial and co-eternal with the Father and the Son. The Father is fully God in himself, the Son born of the Father is fully God. The Holy Spirit, proceeding from the Father and the Son, is fully God . . .

Pope Leo's letter to the Eastern Churches is interesting in two respects. First, he clearly states his personal belief in the procession of the Spirit from the Father and the Son, although he will later prohibit the Franks from the "illicit" addition of the *Filioque* to the Ecumenical Creed. In his "profession of faith" Pope Leo does not distinguish between

---

[2a] *PL* 102, 1030-1032; *Epistola XV seu Symbolum Orthodoxae Fidei Leonis Papae.*

the doctrine of the *Filioque* and its addition to the Creed. Secondly, Pope Leo enunciates quite clearly the belief that everyone must "hold the correct and inviolate faith according to the Holy Roman Catholic and Apostolic Church."

Meanwhile, Patriarch Thomas of Jerusalem had written to Pope Leo III about the incident in Jerusalem. His letter is unfortunately no longer extant. Pope Leo forwarded the letter of the Pilgrim Monks and the letter from Patriarch Thomas to Charlemagne along with an explanatory letter of his own.

> This very year the monks on Mt. Olivet, who are involved in a dispute over the faith, sent us a letter telling of what had happened there. We sent them a Creed of the Orthodox Faith because all should adhere to the right and inviolate faith of this our Holy, Catholic and Apostolic Church. We send this letter referring it to your imperial power. Meanwhile, your faithful servants who were returning from Jerusalem, namely Agamus and Roculphus, brought back to us a letter from Thomas, Patriarch of Jerusalem. Reading it over, we found that we commend them to your piety . . . We, therefore, ask your imperial power to impart judgment over all your faithful subjects, as you are accustomed to do. . ."[3]

Upon receiving the letter from Pope Leo III, along with the other two letters, Charlemagne charged his theologians to prepare a reply to the Greek monks in Jerusalem. It was in response to the controversy at Jerusalem that Theodulf of Orléans wrote his *De Spiritu Sancto* for Charlemagne. It is also possible that the *Libellus de Processione Spiritus Sancti,* often falsely attributed to Alcuin, was written at this time. In November of 809 Charlemagne convoked a council at Aachen at which Theodulf's *De Spiritu Sancto* appears to have been read and to have received imperial sanction.[4]

---

[3]*PL* 129, 1259.

[4]See Hefele-Leclercq, *op. cit.*, III, deuxième partie, p. 1129: "L'écrit de Theodulf fut certainement lut et approuvé au concile d'Aix-la-Chapelle. . ."; see also Hergenröther, *op. cit.*, I, p. 698: "Wahrscheinlich war die Schrift des Theodolphus . . . auf der Synode verlesen und gebilligt."

Theodulf's *De Spiritu Sancto*

The subtitle of Theodulf's *De Spiritu Sancto*[5] quite accurately describes the nature of the work: *Veterum Patrum sententiae, quod a Patre Filioque procedat.* It is simply a collection of patristic texts in support of the Latin doctrine that the Spirit proceeds from the Father and the Son.

It is possible, however, to extract a basic Carolingian theological perspective from this work because the patristic texts are arranged in general around certain theological principles, the most important of which are found in the latter part of *De Spiritu Sancto*. These principles as well as their support are thoroughly Augustinian.

One basic idea permeates the entire work—the idea of the absolute *oneness* of God, an idea which expresses itself in different ways. The emphasis on the *oneness* of God leads to the stress on the inseparability of the nature of the Trinity. These two ideas, according to the Carolingian perspective, demand that there be no difference between the Spirit's relation to the Father and the Spirit's relation to the Son. Ultimately this emphasis leads to the conclusion that the Holy Spirit proceeds from the nature or substance of the Deity.[6]

The proofs that the Spirit proceeds from the Father and the Son come from the Augustinian and post-Augustinian Latin tradition. Since the Spirit is the inspiration of the Father and the Son, and since the Son is the fountain of the Holy Spirit, the Spirit must proceed from the Son. Since the mission of the Holy Spirit is from the Son, then the Spirit must proceed from the Son. Since the Son and the Spirit are in the Father, and since the Spirit proceeds from

---

[5]*PL* 105, 239-276.

[6]*PL* 105, 244: "qui de una natura procedit . . . qui de ipsa unita substantia procedit." These texts are quoted from the pseudo-Athanasian corpus.

God [*Deus*], then the Spirit must also proceed from the Son because the name Son cannot be excluded from God. Since the Spirit "receives" from the Son, then he must proceed from the Son. Since, according to Revelation 22:1, there is a river which proceeds from the throne of God and the Lamb, and since the throne of God symbolizes the Father and the Lamb symbolizes the Son, the river must be the Holy Spirit who proceeds from the Father and the Son. Since the Spirit is "of the Father" and "of the Son," then he must proceed from both. Finally, since the Spirit is inseparable from the Father and the Son, he must proceed from both.

The patristic quotations taken from the works of Augustine are quite lengthy. Eleven columns of *De Spiritu Sancto* come from the works of Augustine. Theodulf quotes from *Contra Maximinum*,[7] from *De Incarnatione Domini*,[8] from Augustine's *Epistola* 118, from *De Civitate Dei*,[9] from the *Tractatus in Joannis Evangelium* and extensively from *De Trinitate*[10]

Although Augustine is the Church Father most often quoted in *De Spiritu Sancto,* Theodulf also quotes texts from other patristic authorities. He quotes at length from the pseudo-Athanasian corpus, including the Athanasian Creed. He also quotes from Cyril of Alexandria, Hilary, Ambrose, Didymus-Jerome, Pope Gregory, Pope Hormisdas, Pope Leo, Isidore of Seville, Prosper,[11] Fulgentius, Vigilius of Thapsus, Proclus,[12] Agnellus, Cassiodorus, and Prudentius.

---

[7] *Contra Maximinum* III, 17 and III, 9.

[8] These quotations, however, are not found in Augustine's *De Incarnatione Domini*.

[9] *De Civitate Dei* 13, 24.

[10] *De Trinitate* I, 4; I, 8; III, prologue; IV, 20; VI, 10, 26.

[11] Theodulf is actually quoting from Julianus Pomerius' *De Vita contemplativa* 1, 18.

[12] The quotation from Proclus, Bishop of Constantinople (434-446), merely affirms the inseparability of the nature of the Trinity. (*PL* 105, 273).

Libellus de Processione Spiritus Sancti

Although the *Libellus de Processione Spiritus Sancti*[13] found its way into the Alcuinian corpus, most scholars do not accept the alleged Alcuinian authorship.[14] All scholars agree that it was written between 800 and 809. From the internal evidence of its polemical tone it would appear that the work was written as a result of the controversy over the *Filioque* between the Frankish monks and the Greeks in Jerusalem.

The first Biblical proof for the *Filioque* doctrine which the author of the *Libellus* brings forth comes from Luke 6:19 which states that "power came forth from him [Christ]." The author of the *Libellus* immediately appeals to the authority of Augustine, stating that "that virtue [power] is the Holy Spirit . . . just as Blessed Augustine affirms in the fifteenth book of *De Trinitate*."[15] The author readily admits that he is "going to use his [Augustine's] words in what follows also in the exposition of this chapter."[16]

The next Biblical proof for the *Filioque* doctrine is that Christ breathed the Spirit on his disciples and hence the Spirit must proceed from the Son. The author of the *Libellus* appeals to Pope Leo, Gregory of Nazianzus, Jerome and Fulgentius to support this uncontested Biblical fact. But again the author's main authority is Augustine. "The blessed and venerable bishop Augustine also" affirms this. The

---

[13]*PL* 101, 64-82.

[14]See Hauck, *op. cit.*, II, p. 347 and Amann, *op. cit.*, p. 182. For an unconvincing defense of Alcuinian authorship see Arthur Kleinclausz, *Alcuin* (Paris, 1948), pp. 204-205.

[15]*PL* 101, 66. The reference is to *De Trinitate* XV, 26. The Latin text of Luke 6:19 is: ". . . quia *virtus* de illo exibat." Augustine did in fact use this text as a proof for the *Filioque*.

[16]*PL* 101, 66.

author of the *Libellus* then quotes from Augustine's *Tractatus in Joannis Evangelium,* after which he turns his attention to Augustine's *De Trinitate.*

> Augustine also in book four of *De Trinitate* in his twenty-first chapter . . . testifies that the Only-Begotten Son of God declares that the Holy Spirit proceeds from him by breathing on the apostles . . . Hence St. Augustine says "we cannot say that the Holy Spirit does not proceed also from the Son" . . . The same distinguished doctor Augustine in the twenty-sixth chapter of the fifteenth book of *De Trinitate* testifies that the Holy Spirit proceeds from the Father and the Son.[17]

What is noteworthy about the methodology of the author of the *Libellus* is that he does not actually begin with Biblical material but rather takes Biblical examples from Augustine and then uses Augustine's interpretation of the Biblical material to support his Biblical proofs. Later in the *Libellus* the author returns to Biblical proofs, again using the same methodology. In this latter part of the work the author seeks to demonstrate that the Spirit is "of the Father and of the Son" and hence must proceed from both. Lengthy quotations from Augustine follow as well as quotations from Pope Leo, Ambrose and Fulgentius.

The final appeal to Biblical texts centers on identifying the sending of the Spirit with the Spirit's eternal procession from both the Father and the Son. The author of the Libellus quotes at length from Augustine's *De Trinitate*[18] and then quotes from Gregory of Nazianzus[19] and Athanasius. One of the quotations from Athanasius is authentic but it does not speak at all about the procession of the Spirit; it simply theologizes concerning the consubstantiality of the Divine Persons, which, for the Carolingians, axiomatically

---

[17]*PL* 101, 68-69.

[18]*De Trinitate* IV, 21.

[19]There is nothing in the quotation from Gregory of Nazianzus which identifies the temporal sending of the Spirit with the Spirit's eternal procession.

implied a procession of the Spirit from both the Father and the Son. The other quotation from Athanasius is from the pseudo-Athanasian Creed.

The author of the *Libellus* then appeals to the authority of the Ecumenical Councils. The Third Ecumenical Council at Ephesus, which was "confirmed by Blessed Pope Celestine with apostolic authority,"[20] accepted as canonical the letter which Cyril of Alexandria wrote to Nestorius, confessing that the Spirit is not alien to the Son "for he is called the Spirit of Truth (and Christ is the Truth), and he flows from him as he also flows from God the Father."[21] The acceptance of Cyril's letter by the Ecumenical Council and the papal confirmation of that council means, according to the author of the *Libellus,* that the Universal Church accepted the doctrine of the Spirit's procession from the Father and the Son.

In his appeal to the Fourth Ecumenical Council the author of the *Libellus* clearly states his view of papal authority. "Most blessed and reverend Leo, Bishop of the Holy See, by whose authority and judgment the Council of Chalcedon was approved and confirmed . . . had *pre-judged* the matter by the Spirit and, as it were, deliberated only to please his brothers."[22] The author of the *Libellus* claims that Pope Leo's letter to Flavian, which was accepted by the Council of Chalcedon, is proof that the Council accepted the doctrine of the procession of the Spirit from the Son. However, all that Pope Leo claims in his letter is that Christ breathed the Holy Spirit on the disciples. For the Carolingians this was the equivalent of stating that the Spirit proceeds from the Son. For the East the statement had nothing whatever to do with the eternal procession of the Spirit.

The author of the *Libellus* arrives most interestingly at the conclusion that the Fifth Ecumenical Council, "the Holy

---

[20]*PL* 101, 70.

[21]*Ibid.*

[22]*PL* 101, 71.

Council of Constantinople, also believes and professes that the Holy Spirit proceeds from the Father and the Son."[23] The author's reasoning is as follows. Since the Council of Ephesus accepted Cyril's letter which stated that the Spirit is poured forth from the Son, and since the Council of Chalcedon and the Council of Constantinople confirmed the ecumenicity of the Council of Ephesus, it therefore follows that the Council of Constantinople, which, as all previous Councils, received its ultimate authority through papal confirmation, "believes and professes that the Holy Spirit proceeds from the Father and the Son."

There is another reason why the author of the *Libellus* claims that the Council of Constantinople accepted the *Filioque* doctrine. The first session of the Council of Constantinople decreed the following:

> We further declare that we hold fast to the decrees of the Four Councils, and *in every way* follow the Holy Fathers—Athanasius, Hilary, Basil, Gregory of Nyssa, Ambrose, Theophilus, John Chrysostom, Cyril, *Augustine,* Proclus, and Leo.[24]

According to the perspective of the author of the *Libellus,* the Fifth Ecumenical Council accepted *"in every way"* the Holy Father Augustine. If it accepted and followed Augustine *"in every way,"* then it must uphold the teaching that the Spirit proceeds from the Father and the Son. He writes that

> Blessed Augustine, whose authority and doctrine Pope Gelasius with apostolic authority and the above-mentioned Council of Constantinople decreed should be received and followed by the Universal Church, testifies in chapter twenty-six of the fifteenth book of *De Trinitate* that the same Holy Spirit proceeds from the Father and the Son.[25]

The author of the *Libellus* later exclaims: "Let those who strive to deny that the Holy Spirit proceeds from the Son

---

[23] *PL* 101, 72.
[24] *PL* 101, 73.
[25] *PL* 101, 75.

. . . let them hear what Blessed Augustine says in *De Trinitate*."[26]

Faithful to the post-Augustinian Latin tradition, the author of the *Libellus* ends his work with a quotation from the Athanasian Creed: "Let him who wishes to be saved, think thus of the Trinity."[27] The author, claiming that the *Filioque* doctrine neither obliterates the Trinity nor separates its substantial unity, states that this belief is "the certain and unchanging rule of Catholic Faith."[28]

The uniqueness of the *Libellus de Processione Spiritus Sancti* lies in its method of appeal to the Ecumenical Councils, a method which, according to the author's perspective, allows for the ecumenical authority of the works of Augustine.

Although it is possible to interpret the acts of the first session of the Fifth Ecumenical Council as endorsing the works of Augustine, it is also possible, and historically more accurate, to interpret the statement in the light of the concluding phrase—"and their writings on the true faith." According to the latter interpretation, only the works of Augustine which coincide with the "true faith" could receive ecumenical sanction.

From a strictly historical perspective it must be stated that the majority of the Fathers of the Fifth Ecumenical Council were not even acquainted with the works of Augustine. There was only one aspect of the thought of Augustine which interested Emperor Justinian (527-565). Justinian, in an attempt to bring the Monophysites back to Orthodoxy, wanted to condemn posthumously certain works of Theodore of Mopsuestia (d. 428), Ibas of Edessa (d. 457), and Theodoret of Cyrus (d. 466) for Nestorian tendencies. But Justinian met with certain opposition from those who claimed that no one could condemn the dead, especially if

---

[26] *PL* 101, 76.
[27] *PL* 101, 82.
[28] *PL* 101, 82.

they had died in harmony with the Church. Complicating the matter was the fact that Theodoret and Ibas had been declared Orthodox by the Council of Chalcedon. An African priest by the name of Mocianus provided Justinian with texts from the works of Augustine which stated that the Church had the power to excommunicate a heretic posthumously. Although some of the texts came from the pseudo-Augustinian corpus, the text from Augustine's *Epistola* 185,4 was authentic.[29] It was this aspect of Augustine's thought which became useful to Justinian and the decree of the Fifth Ecumenical Council acknowledges its debt to Augustine in this regard.

> Several letters of Augustine, of most religious memory, who shone forth resplendent among the African bishops, were read, showing that it was quite right that heretics should be anathematized after death. And this ecclesiastical tradition, the other most reverend bishops of Africa have preserved.[30]

---

[29] Augustine's view had been canonized in Canon 81 of the *Codex canonum ecclesiae Africana* (PL 67, 206).

[30] *NPNF*, XIV, p. 309. This statement is not quite accurate, for Pontianus of Carthage had opposed Justinian, claiming that neither an Emperor nor any man had the right to judge the dead.

CHAPTER VI

The Frankish Envoys and Pope Leo III

Smaragdus' Letter to Pope Leo III

After the Council of Aachen had sanctioned the *Filioque* addition to the Ecumenical Creed and had presumably given *imperial* sanction to Theodulf's *De Spiritu Sancto* and perhaps also to the *Libellus de Processione Spiritus Sancti,* Charlemagne sought papal approval of his Council. He therefore commissioned Abbot Smaragdus (d. 840) to write an introductory letter to Pope Leo III (795-816) explaining the decision of the Council of Aachen. Smaragdus was also commissioned to head a Frankish delegation to Rome.

Smaragdus begins his letter to Pope Leo III,[1] written in the name of Charlemagne, with a description of the recent controversy on the procession of the Holy Spirit.

---

[1] PL 98, 923-929; *Epistola XIX ad Leonem Papam, a Zmaragdo abbate lita,* anno 809.

> The question which has lately arisen about the procession of the Holy Spirit was for a long time very diligently treated by the Holy Fathers. But because it was being neglected for a long time, it has remained as though not treated of old, but it has suddenly come to light like something hidden. As a faithful believer, I do not doubt that this [new controversy] was divinely inspired. Because . . . this question has not been discussed for a long time, Almighty God wished to excite the hearts of pastors . . . so that they can remove the sluggishness of neglect . . . Therefore, let sluggish inertia be put far from pastors . . . let soft sleep change to severe and profitable vigils spent in *reading* so that the rich soil of the Church, sown with the seed of the Doctors, can render fruit a hundred-fold to the Almighty.[2]

For Smaragdus the controversy on the procession of the Holy Spirit is a result of Divine initiative and it demands decisive action on the part of the Church. Smaragdus appeals to Biblical and patristic authority to show that the action of the Council of Aachen was based on Catholic truth. Since the Scripture teaches that the "Spirit of the Father is in the Son and is the Spirit of both," therefore the Spirit must proceed from both. Since Christ poured forth the Spirit on the disciples, the Spirit must proceed from the Son. Smaragdus also claims that Isaiah 11:4[3] teaches that the Spirit is the mouth of the Son and hence proceeds from the Son. His final appeal to Biblical material concerns itself with John 15:26: "The Lord himself testifies that the Spirit proceeds from the Father."[4] But "the book of Job, made sacred by the mouth of the Lord, testifies that the same Spirit proceeds from the Son when it says: 'Hearken to the thunder of his voice and the rumbling that comes from his mouth'."[5] Smaragdus' interpretation of this text is taken from Pope Gregory.

---

[2] *PL* 98, 923-925.

[3] Isaiah 11:4: "He shall smite the earth with the rod of his mouth, and with the breath of his lips he shall slay the wicked."

[4] *PL* 98, 923.

[5] Job 37:2; *PL* 98, 923.

Blessed Gregory, in explaining the verse of Job mentioned above, says: "The Only-Begotten Son can be designated as the mouth of God. The Holy Spirit can be called the sound of his mouth. The sound then proceeds from the mouth of the Lord when his consubstantial Spirit, coming to us *through the Son*, assumed the deafness of our insensibility."[6]

In his appeal to patristic authority Smaragdus quotes from the pseudo-Athanasian corpus, from Cyril of Alexandria, from Ambrose, and from Augustine's *Contra Maximinum* and *De Trinitate*. Smaragdus concludes that "fed on the statements of the Divine books and overwhelmed by the weight of many Orthodox witnesses, no unfriendly person can resist the truth."[7]

This introductory letter by Smaragdus had no impact on Pope Leo III. Indeed, the work was quite unnecessary because Pope Leo III did not have to be convinced of the validity of the *doctrine* of the *Filioque* which he himself accepted. What Pope Leo III would not accept was the addition of the *Filioque* to the Ecumenical Creed.

The Meeting between the Franks and Pope Leo III

The Frankish delegation, headed by Smaragdus, met with Pope Leo in 810. Smaragdus recorded the dialogue to the best of his ability, a dialogue of such importance for the Byzantine-Carolingian Triadological controversy that it deserves to be quoted at length.[8]

When the . . . envoys had read the testimony[9] in

---

[6]*PL* 98, 923.

[7]*PL* 98, 929.

[8]*PL* 102, 971-976; *Acta Collationis Romae, descripta a Smaragdo abbate sancti Michaelis*. The text was translated into English by Raymond Ciuba and the author.

[9]This presumably includes the acts of the Council of Aachen, Smaragdus' letter, and perhaps other Carolingian works on the subject of the procession of the Holy Spirit.

detail and were given a hearing most diligently by the apostolic Lord, he spoke thus: This is how I think, and I hold to it firmly, along with *these* writers and the authority of the Holy Scriptures. If anyone wants to think or teach otherwise in this matter, I shall defend his right; and unless he change his mind, and choose to adhere to this way of thinking, I shall entirely abandon the contrary point of view. Having said these things, I know that some are better at dialogue than debate; unless their train of thought or arrangement of words is just so, they cannot remember what to say. When the conference had reached a point where the dispute was already more certain, the conversation took place. *If this was not the exact way of speech,* inasmuch as I am able to remember, it is nevertheless the way of thinking, and the ultimate conclusion of the newest definitions.

Envoys: Since it is indeed as you say, that this most certainly be believed, and therefore immutably held, and therefore faithfully defended wherever necessary, should it not also be taught to those who are ignorant and be confirmed for those who know that we may adhere to it more attentively?

Pope Leo: Yes.

Envoys: If that is so, can anyone who does not know this or does not believe this possibly be saved?

Pope Leo: Anyone who can attain to this by simple thinking and know it, or who does know it, and will not believe, cannot be saved. There are many things, of which this is one, which are deep mysteries and sacraments of the Holy Faith, which many are able to search and attain. Many people, whether by age or by intelligence hindered, are not capable. And therefore, as we have already said, one who can and will not, cannot be saved.

Envoys: If this is so, or better, since it is so, since it is not allowed not to believe, and since it is not allowed to teach by being silent about the matter, why is it not permissible to sing it, and to teach it by singing?

Pope Leo: It is allowed, I tell you, to sing it in teaching, and to teach it in singing. *But it is not allowed to insert it illicitly,* whether in writing or singing, in places where it is prohibited.

Envoys: Since we all know this, that in writing or singing the Creed, it is wrong to say or to omit anything, since those who established the Creed did not insert it, as they, and the following major Councils —the fourth at Chalcedon and the fifth and sixth at Constantinople, prohibited the creation of a new Creed by anyone for any reason, need, or soul-saving devotion, and forbade also any addition, subtraction, or alteration in the old wording—it is not necessary to dwell upon these facts too long. But this I ask, and I beseech you: Is it good to believe this; is it as good for us today to believe and sing it, as it would have been if it had been inserted of old?

Pope Leo: Certainly it is good, very good, for *it is forbidden not to believe such a great doctrine of the faith,* for anyone who is able to attain to it.

Envoys: Then it is not good to say that the authors did not write it so, *if by adding only four syllables we clarify* such a necessary mystery of faith *for all succeeding centuries?*

Pope Leo: Just as I dare not say that they did not do what they did well, since undoubtedly they omitted other things as well, even though they knew them, and they acted upon divine illumination rather than by human wisdom, even so I dare not say also that they knew this less than we know it. If they considered it, why did they omit it? Or why, having omitted it, did they prohibit anything else from being added? See how I feel toward you and your people. *I shall not say that I prefer myself to the Fathers. And far be it from me to count myself their equal.*

Envoys: Indeed, far be it from us, Father, by God's protection, to think or say anything, whether being puffed up with pride, or provoked by the desire for human praise in matters divine. *If we presume not only to prefer ourselves to the Fathers, but even to equate ourselves to them,* it is only because of the way of our times. Being patient and charitable toward the weakness of our brothers, we seek and labor for one thing: that, *since the end of the world is coming,* when the times are dangerous as predicted, we may be able to witness well to our brothers. We are eager to restore the faithful in the Lord to the mysteries of faith; and, therefore, since we have found that the Creed was sung in such a manner by some, and since we feel that it touches the faith of the Church, we realize that very many learned men, and men of all future ages, must be instructed about such a mystery, if it is held so, and some will not learn it unless it is sung. It seemed better to us to teach men by singing rather than silently to leave them untaught. If your Paternity knew how many thousands of people know this today because of the singing, who would never have known except by the singing, perhaps you would agree with us and be pleased to consent to its singing.

Pope Leo: For the time being I will agree with you. However, I ask you to answer this: Are all the mysteries of the faith, which are not contained in the Creed, and without which no one who is able to know them can possibly call himself a Catholic, are they all to be inserted in the Creed, and added to the Creed, not for the advantage of those who do not know, but just as anyone is pleased to add?

Envoys: Certainly not. Not all things are equally necessary.

Pope Leo: Even if not all things are necessary, there are certainly many things like these, which must be believed by all who are able, or else they cannot be Catholics.

Envoys: Can you give us an example of something, not necessarily so sublime, but at least similar to the present matter, which is lacking in the Creed?

Pope Leo: Certainly. I shall give you many examples.

Envoys: First give us just one, and, if necessary, add another.

Pope Leo: Because the present question is being treated in a friendly manner and because the question is for the good of both parties (and would that as often as something of this sort is treated by major or minor clerics for the good of Catholics, it would be handled as peacefully without perverse intention), lest we speak rashly of mysteries that deserve great reverence, let time be allotted for consideration, and I will speak what the Lord will grant me.

[After a suitable overnight delay]

Pope Leo: Is it more salutary to believe or dangerous not to believe that the Holy Spirit proceeds from the Son just as from the Father than that the Son was born the Wisdom of God from the Wisdom of God,

the Truth of God from the Truth of God, because
God is essentially Truth, although it is agreed that
this was not written by the Holy Fathers into the
Creed. If then, these two points, as it becomes the
wise, are established in so friendly a disputation,
that you feel with us and know that so many earlier
Catholic Fathers either did not insert the doctrine
under discussion into the creeds or prevented other
things from being inserted, as was said previously—if,
I say, the Fathers omitted things not from ignorance,
not from future negligent oversight, and prohibited
the omitted part from being inserted, we gladly
refrain...

Envoys: It is not necessary, I say, to labor the point
whether we do not know what we know because
whatever others know from any source, we know,
for God is the author, or we are able to know, even
if we do not know.

Pope Leo: This is something we marvel at that you,
who can rest without labor, strive not to rest.

Envoys: We do not work in order to avoid rest but
lest, through laziness we lose the reward of pious
work, and avoiding more diligent inquiry and
declining sharp debate, we consider the gain which
is acquired thereby in the heart of those who seek,
greater than the harm done in the heart of those
who have added, as if despisers of the works of the
Fathers would arise through insolence. For it is one
thing to despise good things by passing over them
through pride; it is another to *make good things
even better through good will.*

Pope Leo: Even if it is good to discuss in some cases,
nevertheless there should not be discussion everywhere. Much evidence could be added on this point,

but the matter is clear. How much better it would be for each person to strive to render some good in a useful way. Or if by chance he strives to make the good better, *let him in the first place take care and exert great effort lest by rashly presuming beyond what he ought and by corrupting what was good in itself, he renders it harmful.* . . . This perhaps touches you, if you do not disdain to listen . . . not even a wise man can sing without going wrong or by singing teach anyone as you wish. And while you choose to help many by a path other than the one you ought to take, you send no one on this path whom you would not harm. . . . This defense of yours, or if it may be said, this refusal, does not look this way or that way because the same Fathers in their decision neither decreed nor sanctioned that someone well-disposed might presume it [i.e. to add, subtract or alter the Creed], or someone not ill-disposed, but they decreed simply that *no one* might.

Envoys: Did you not give permission for singing this Creed in the Church?

Pope Leo: I gave permission for the singing of the Creed but not for the adding, subtracting or altering of the Creed while it is sung. . . . For we do not sing it [in Rome] but read the Creed and in reading it we teach. *Nor do we presume in our reading or teaching to add anything to the Creed by insertion.* . . . We take care that competent persons do this at opportune times or places.

Envoys: Therefore, as I see it, this is decreed by your Paternity. That first the point which is being discussed [i.e. the *Filioque*] be removed from the Creed. And then at last it may be learned and taught licitly by anyone either in singing or in handing it down.

Pope Leo: Without doubt, it is so decided on our part. We persuade you in every way that you would agree, too, on your part.

Envoys: When those things you wish have been removed, then it is good that the Creed be sung.

Pope Leo: Good indeed. But this we say not by way of ordering it but by permitting it as before, because just as then so now, too, if it is handled sincerely, it can be useful to the needy.

Envoys: Because as you say—and you speak truly—it is good to sing the Creed, if a sermon full of true faith is taken from its midst, will the same sermon be condemned by everyone as if it were contrary to the faith? What kind of advice will you give so that it will not have this outcome?

Pope Leo: If I had been asked before, I would have replied definitely that it [i.e. the *Filioque*] should not be inserted.... But now ... it seems to me that both things can be done:[10] that gradually in the Palace the custom of singing the Creed can be dispensed with because it is not sung in our Holy Church.... If you will dispense with it, all will dispense with it. And so, perhaps, in so far as can be done, both things could be dispensed with.

The dialogue speaks for itself. There are, however, a few details which deserve to be stressed. Pope Leo expressly states that he does not "prefer himself to the Fathers" and does not "count himself" their equal, an interesting remark in the light of later papal claims. Pope Leo upbraids

---

[10] The removal of the *Filioque* from the Creed and the ending of the singing of the Creed.

the presumption of the Franks who consider themselves wiser than the Fathers of the Ecumenical Councils. Although Pope Leo accepted the *doctrine* of the *Filioque,* the addition of the *Filioque* to the Ecumenical Creed is "illicit" and the Frankish arrogance of presuming to make what is "good even better" could result in "corrupting" what was already good. Although the "friendly" atmosphere of the discussion is often stressed, Pope Leo is actually quite stern with the Franks and at times appears quite exasperated by their arrogance and excessive zeal. Although Pope Leo had previously given the Franks permission to sing the Creed, he now uses this discussion as a pretext for not only removing the *Filioque* from the Creed but also for dispensing with the custom of singing the Creed.

Pope Leo's response to the Franks did not end with his order that the Franks remove the *Filioque* from the Ecumenical Creed. He took other measures. He considered the problem so serious that he had "two silver shields" engraved with the original Nicene-Constantinopolitan Creed in both Greek and Latin and then placed on each side of the Confession of St. Peter. He did this, according to Anastasius Bibliothecarius,[11] "for the love he bore to the Orthodox Faith and out of his care for its preservation." Photius refers to these shields, even though he mistakenly thought that both shields were engraved in Greek. The existence of these shields is confirmed by the later testimony of Peter Damian,[12] Peter Lombard,[13] and Peter Abelard.[14] Recent historical research has also confirmed the historicity of these shields.[15]

The Franks, however, did not heed the order of Pope

---

[11]*PL* 128, 1238.
[12]*PL* 145, 635.
[13]*PL* 192, 552.
[14]*PL* 178, 1073.

[15]See Vittorio Peri, "Il Simbolo Epigrafico di S. Leone III nelle Basiliche Romane dei SS. Pietro e Paolo," *Rivista di Archeologia Christiana,* **XLV** (1969), 191-221.

Leo and the Carolingian "assault" carried the interpolated Creed with it in its missionary work among the Slavs, culminating in Photius' sharp criticism of both the *Filioque* doctrine and its addition to the Ecumenical Creed.

CHAPTER VII

Photius' Encyclical

The Franks had ignored Pope Leo's request and continued to use the *Filioque* in the Ecumenical Creed. Although the former political unity of the Carolingian Empire began to disintegrate after the death of Charlemagne in 814, the Franks maintained another type of unity, the unity of the Frankish-Latin Church. A new power struggle soon emerged among the Franks, the Roman See and Byzantium, the object of which was the Christianization of the Slavs and jurisdictional control over the Bulgars.

The Christianization of the Slavs

Christian missionary work among the Slavs began under Emperor Heraclius (610-641),[1] who had asked Pope Hon-

---

[1] According to Emperor Constantine Porphyrogenitus' (913-959) *De Administrando Imperio*. A letter of Pope Agatho (678-681) mentions that the Roman See was Christianizing the Slavs (*PG* 87, 1226). There is no

orius I (625-638) to send Roman missionaries to the southern Slavs, presumably the Croats.² Frankish missionary work among the Slavs began after Charlemagne devastated the Avars in 795-796. It was Patriarch Paulinus who, under the inspiration of Alcuin's missionary zeal,³ used his See as an operational base to reach "this barbarous and unreasonable, indeed idiotic people, who lacked even the most basic spiritual culture."⁴

The rivalry among the Franks, the Roman See, and Byzantium concerned the Christianization of the Bulgars, a tribe which had settled in parts of Illyricum in 679 and had become gradually Slavicized. The Bulgars were a constant threat to Byzantium. Emperor Constantine V (741-775), after eight military campaigns against the Bulgars, could not destroy them, and two Byzantine Emperors died in wars against the Bulgars.⁵ When Boris of Bulgaria agreed to accept Christianity, the Franks, the Roman See and Byzantium rivaled with one another for jurisdictional control of the new converts.

> Whereas the Bulgarian problem was for the Franks and for Rome only a matter of prestige, it was for the Byzantines a matter of life and death, for Byzantium could not possibly permit another power, whether political or cultural, to settle at its very doors.⁶

---

reason to dismiss the evidence from *De Administrando Imperio* because Pope Honorius was on good terms with the Emperor and the territory belonged at this time to the jurisdiction of the Roman See.

²See Francis Dvornik, "Byzantium, Rome, the Franks, and the Christianization of the Southern Slavs," *Cyrillo-Methodiana,* ed. by Hellmann, Olesch, Stasiewski, Zagiba (Köln, 1964), p. 88.

³See Alcuin's letters 60 (*MGH, Epistolae* IV, p. 104), 95 (p. 139), 96 (p. 140), and 98 (p. 142).

⁴Quoted from Giannoni, *op. cit.,* p. 42. The quotation is Paulinus'.

⁵Emperor Nicephorus (802-811) was killed in battle against the Bulgars and Emperor Michael I (811-813) died as the result of a war against the Bulgars.

⁶Francis Dvornik, *The Photian Schism* (Cambridge: University Press, 1948), p. 94.

As a result of the Moravian-Byzantine military alliance, Boris of Bulgaria renounced his intended Bulgarian-Frankish alliance and consented to be baptized by the Byzantines.

Boris was baptized by Patriarch Photius (858-867; 878-886) and was so deeply impressed by the Patriarchal ceremonies that he wanted a Patriarch for his newly converted people. The Byzantines refused to give the Bulgars their own Patriarchate and then Boris, always realizing the importance of being independent of Byzantium, sent letters to Louis the German and Pope Nicholas I (858-867), complaining that the Byzantines would not only not grant him a Patriarchate but also refused to permit certain Bulgarian customs. Pope Nicholas responded by sending two Roman Bishops, Paul of Populonia and Formosus of Porto, to Bulgaria with Roman missionaries.

> The papal embassy was received in Bulgaria with extreme satisfaction; and Boris delighted every time the Pope's gracious letter was read out to him. All his doubts were cleared and all the problems he had raised were solved: he was pleased that his Bulgars—men and women—could go on wearing breeches, without the fear of committing a mortal sin; he could henceforth take his bath on Wednesdays and Fridays and go to communion wearing his belt . . . Though, after all, he might as well do without a Patriarch, if it came to that, and be content with an archbishop, since the Pope had told him that it came more or less to the same thing. He was especially pleased to hear that the Patriarch of Constantinople, who had impressed him so deeply, was only a sham Patriarch, not in the same class as the Patriarchs of Rome, Alexandria and Antioch.[7]

The Roman missionaries asked Boris to dismiss the Byzantine missionaries. The Byzantines were unable to take any military action against the Bulgars because there was an internal revolution in Byzantium[8] and Bulgaria had strengthened its border defenses. Upon returning to Con-

---

[7]Dvornik, *op. cit.*, p. 114.

[8]Caesar Bardas had been murdered by Basil the Macedonian (867-886). ee J. B. Bury, *A History of the Eastern Roman Empire* (London, 1912), . 170 f.

stantinople, the expelled Byzantine missionaries complained about certain "suspicious" customs and doctrines of the Franks. They explained that the Bulgars used milk and cheese during Lent, that they forbade married men from becoming priests, and that they permitted only bishops to administer confirmation. But most importantly, they were surprised that the Franks were using an interpolated text of the Nicene-Constantinopolitan Creed which contained the *Filioque*.

The Encyclical

Patriarch Photius considered the *Filioque* addition to the Creed as a most serious problem. But he also seems to consider these disciplinary differences as serious, for it was at this time that he wrote his famous Encyclical[9] to the "archepiscopal thrones" of the East. But Photius is remarkably inconsistent at this point. In his Encyclical he interprets the Canons of the Sixth Ecumenical Council, better known as the Quinisext Council, as having "ecumenical" validity, for he attacks the Western customs by appealing to these canons. But in 861 or 862 in his second letter[10] to Pope Nicholas I Photius explicitly refers to these different customs, arguing that neither East nor West should impose their customs on each other. Thus, in this letter to Pope Nicholas he did not interpret the Canons of the Quinisext Council as being "ecumenically" binding on the West. The change in Photius' perspective may very well have been prompted by Pope Nicholas' *Responsa ad consulta Bulgarorum*[11] which

---

[9]*PG* 102, 721-741.
[10]*PG* 102, 593-617.
[11]*PL* 119, 978-1017.

was quite anti-Greek in content.¹² Photius may only have been attempting to protect the "Byzantine customs" by appealing to these canons as "ecumenical."¹³ Nevertheless, this does not alter the fact that Photius was inconsistent.

The custom of fasting on Saturday was uncanonical and Photius appeals to the sixty-fourth apostolic canon¹⁴ and the Sixth Ecumenical Council.¹⁵ Photius thinks "there is no need to condemn them by reciting canons" for the fact that they separate the first week of Lent from the other weeks

---

¹²See G. T. Dennis, "The 'anti-Greek' Character of the *Responsa ad Bulgaros* of Nicholas I," *Orientalia Christiana periodica*, XXIV (Rome, 1958), 165-174.

¹³By relying so heavily on the Canons of the Quinisext Council in his Encyclical Photius indirectly opened himself to what Hergenröther terms "eine offenbare Lüge." In his earlier letter to Nicholas, in which Photius explained the circumstances surrounding his elevation to the episcopacy, Photius claimed that the Canon of Sardica which Pope Nicholas accused Photius of violating had not been received in Constantinople. But Canon II of the Quinisext Council accepted the "holy canons" of Sardica. Dvornik's interpretation seems accurate: "as to the canons of Sardica, Photius never pretended that his Church did not know them. All he implied was (that) the tenth canon... had not been carried into practice by the Church of Constantinople, as evidenced by the appointments of Tarasius and Nicephorus." Dvornik, *op. cit.*, p. 92.

¹⁴*PG* 102, 733; no. 29. The sixty-fourth canon, often numbered as canon sixty-six, as quoted by Photius is: "If any cleric be found to fast on Saturday or Sunday, except one Saturday only, let him be deposed. If he is a layman, let him be separated from communion."

¹⁵*PG* 102, 733; no. 30. The fifty-fifth canon as quoted by Photius is: "Because it has come to our attention that those who live in Rome fast on Saturdays in Lent, contrary to ecclesiastical custom and tradition, the Holy Synod decrees that also throughout the Roman Church that canon shall stand which says..." Photius then quotes the "sixty-fourth" canon of the apostolic canons. Although the canons of the Sixth Ecumenical Council were accepted in the East, the Western Church rejected them from the very beginning. The canons of the Sixth Ecumenical Council (680-681) were actually the canons of the Quinisext Council (692) which met eleven years after the Sixth Ecumenical Council and at which the Western Church was barely represented. When the canons of the Quinisext Council were sent to Pope Sergius I (687-701), he refused to sign them, claiming that they were "invalid" and contained "new errors." Only later did the Roman Church accept the canons of the Sixth Ecumenical Council and only those canons which did not contradict Roman practice.

by allowing the eating of dairy products because "even to make mention of those things surpasses the height of anyone's impiety."[16] Photius' main consideration on these minor issues is that "the neglect of even slight traditions can lead to contempt for all doctrine."[17] Photius responds to the fact that they forbid married men from becoming priests by appealing to the fourth canon of the Council of Gangra and to the thirteenth canon of the Sixth Ecumenical Council.[18] That they re-anoint those already chrismated by priests evokes a brief theology of the priesthood from Photius:

> They said it was not lawful for priests to consecrate the baptized with oil, for by law this has been granted to bishops alone. Whence is that law? Who is the legislator? One of the Apostles? Or one of the Fathers? Or one of the Councils? Where did the council take place? When was it called? By whose votes and

---

[16]*PG* 102, 736; no. 32.

[17]*PG* 102, 724; no. 5.

[18]*PG* 102, 733; no. 31. The fourth canon of the Council of Gangra (between 350 and 380) as quoted by Photius states: "If any priest who is married decides that he ought not to communicate when he celebrates the liturgy, let him be anathema." The thirteenth canon of the Quinisext Council as quoted by Photius states: "Since we know that in the Roman church in place of this canon the following practice has prevailed—that those who were to be advanced to the diaconate or priesthood should promise that they would no longer live with their wives—we, observing the ancient canon of apostolic perfection and rank, wish the marriage of those in Holy Orders to be firm and stable from this time forward, not at all dissuading them from intercourse with their wives or depriving them of this at convenient times. Therefore, if anyone has been found worthy to be ordained subdeacon, deacon, or priest, let him not be prevented from assuming such a rank if he lives with his legitimate wife. Neither at the time of his ordination let any promise be demanded that he at all abstain from intercourse with his legitimate wife, so that we would not afflict marriage, instituted by God and honored by his presence, with shame. The Gospel says: 'What God has joined together, let no man put asunder'. And the Apostle teaches: 'Marriage is honorable and an undefiled marriage bed'. And, 'You have married a wife. Do not seek a divorce'. If anyone, then, contrary to apostolic canons, incites any of those who are in orders—priests, deacons, or subdeacons—to abstain from intercourse with a legitimate wife, let him be deposed. Similarly, if any priest or deacon casts out his wife on the pretext of piety or religion, let him be separated; if he persists, let him be deposed."

favor was it approved? A priest may not anoint the baptized with oil? Then certainly do not let the priest baptize or offer sacrifice. Let him return to the lay state. He is not a full priest. He who consecrates the Body of the Lord and the Blood of Christ and sanctifies those who were once initiated into the sacred mysteries, how can it be that the same priest, when he anoints with oil, does not sanctify the initiate? The priest baptizes. He confers the gift on the baptized. By what reasoning will you deprive him of the sign and seal of that purification which he confers?[19]

But it is clear that Photius considers the above-mentioned problems of a disciplinary rather than a doctrinal nature. The most serious problem, a problem of a doctrinal nature, is that the Franks have interpolated the "Holy and Sacred Creed, which has been confirmed by all the Ecumenical Councils."[20] Photius states emphatically that the "blasphemy against the Holy Spirit, or rather against the entire Holy Trinity, would suffice without a second blasphemy for striking them with a thousand anathemas, *even if all the other charges did not exist.*"[21] That Photius considered the *Filioque* as *the* serious issue is clear from his above-quoted statement, from his later controversy with the West which concentrates only on this triadological issue, and from the Encyclical's preoccupation with this problem. The greatest part of the Encyclical consists of "brief and incomplete"[22] refutations of the *Filioque*.

The embryonic stage of Photius' triadological thought begins with this Encyclical. It appears that Photius at this time had no "Latin sources" to utilize; his analysis of the *Filioque* originates in certain "logical" conclusions which he believed must follow if one accepted the doctrine that the Spirit proceeds from the Father and the Son.

Photius immediately perceives that the *Filioque* implies

---

[19]*PG* 102, 725; no. 7.
[20]*PG* 102, 725; no. 8.
[21]*PG* 102, 736; no. 33.
[22]*PG* 102, 732; no. 23.

two principles in the Trinity and asks how any Christian could possibly admit "two causes in the Holy Trinity?" Such would lower Christian theology to the level of Greek mythology. If the Spirit proceeds from the Father and the Son, then the Spirit must be further removed from the Father than the Son is and must be distinguished by more properties than the Son, a view which, according to Photius, approaches the Macedonian heresy. If the Spirit proceeds from the Father and the Son, then the Spirit is the only Person of the Holy Trinity with a plural principle. If there is a procession from the Son, why then can there not be another procession from that procession? Photius maintains that if the substance or nature is the principle of procession, then not only must the Spirit proceed from himself but there should also be a procession of the Father from that nature. Photius also claims that the Son, according to the logics of the *Filioque,* should be begotten by the Father and the Spirit. If God the Father is perfect, then the procession of the Spirit from the Father must be perfect. If this procession is perfect, then what is the possible value in the procession from the Son? Is it not superfluous? If the Spirit proceeds from both, then it would appear that the Spirit is excluded from that common life from which the Spirit proceeds. And, finally, Photius maintains that the very essence of Christian triadology is that either something is common to all Three Persons or else it is the property of One of the Persons. The procession of the Spirit cannot be common. If it is, then it is not a procession of a Person.

Photius is most concerned about the origin of the *Filioque* doctrine.

> Where have you learned this fact which you assert? In what Gospel have you found this word? To what Council belongs such blasphemy? Who will not stop his ears at this enormous blasphemy? It stands in battle, as it were, against the Gospels. It takes up arms against the Holy Councils and falsifies the Blessed Fathers— the great Athanasius; Gregory, hymned as the personification of theology; Basil, that royal robe of the Church; and Chrysostom, the golden mouth of the world, that sea of wisdom. Why should I

name this one or that one? This blasphemy, which declares war on God, is armed against all the Holy Prophets together, the Apostles, the priests, martyrs, and even the voice of the Lord himself.[23]

At the end of his Encyclical Photius calls for the immediate convocation of an Ecumenical Council to settle these problems. Photius requests that the representatives be given "wide powers" so the matter can be decided quickly and decisively.[24]

---

[23]*PG* 102, 728-729; no. 15 and 16.

[24]This council did meet but all that is really known about it is that it condemned Pope Nicholas and that at the last session Louis II was allowed the title "Emperor." Cyril Mango believes that one of the extant homilies of Photius was given at the conclusion of this Council. See the conclusions of this study.

CHAPTER VIII

The Latin Response to Photius' Encyclical

The Response of Pope Nicholas

Papal legates, waiting on the Bulgarian-Byzantine border, were refused entrance into Byzantine territory for not signing a condemnation of Frankish practices and for not recognizing Photius as the legitimate Patriarch. A condemnatory letter from the Emperor to Boris of Bulgaria, along with a list of Greek charges against the Franks, were handed over to the papal legates by Boris and then given to Pope Nicholas. It is reasonable to conclude that Photius' Encyclical was *not* one of the documents.[1]

---

[1] The reasons for so concluding are: 1) Photius sent his Encyclical to the "archepiscopal thrones" of the East and there was much in the letter which he probably did not want Pope Nicholas to find out about; 2) Pope Nicholas in his letter to Hincmar never refers to Photius' Encyclical but rather to the writings of the Greek Emperors; and 3) the replies of Aeneas and Ratramnus are specifically addressed to the Emperors and not Photius.

Not knowing that a Council was condemning him in Constantinople in 867, Pope Nicholas, upon receiving the charges, decided to enlist the support of the Carolingian theologians. Pope Nicholas wrote to Hincmar of Rheims (d. 882),[2] appointing him the "executor of all those things which this letter contains." After relating all the events which led up to the Greek attack on "Western" tradition, Pope Nicholas claims that the "whole Western Church" is under attack by the Greek Emperors.

> For it is ridiculous and an utterly abominable disgrace for us in our times to permit the Holy Church of God to be falsely accused, or those traditions which we received of old from our fathers to be broken at the whim of persons who are ever in error. With the help of divine power we shall... not fail to act; and when the opportunity is given by heaven, we will not hold our peace against them....
>
> It is very fitting, however, that you, following the custom of our fathers, be found working with us..."[3]

Pope Nicholas informs Hincmar that he is

> to send to our office writings divinely inspired by your wisdom for refuting and striking with brave invective the very great insanity of those same leaders. *On receiving these, we can send them together with other statements* of our own to confound their madness so that when the enemy realizes we feel alike, they may not lyingly claim that we are trying to avenge injuries done to ourselves alone. When they see us advance together in concerted battle, as it were, against them and thus clearly understand that there are also other lovers of Christ and haters of their wickedness, the mouths of those speaking iniquities will be completely stopped.[4]

Hincmar is to inform the other Carolingian archbishops of this matter and to make sure that they "discuss the matters... *and supply us with what they have arrived at.*"[5]

---

[2] *MGH, Epistolae* VI, 601-609.
[3] *MGH*, VI, 604.
[4] *MGH*, VI, 608.
[5] *MGH*, VI, 608-609.

The papal letter to Hincmar was written in late October of 867. In December of the same year Hincmar sent a letter to Odo, Bishop of Beauvais,[6] which presumably was similar to the one he sent to the other archbishops.

> So, let each of you who has Metropolitan rank join with his brothers and the bishops under him and expend diligent care on these matters. Let him strive to find out what is needed to oppose these hateful lies and take care to forward his findings as soon as possible to our office . . . When we receive them, we will be able to send them with our other usual observations to confound their insane charges . . . Therefore, dear brothers, according to the recommendation of the Apostolic See, endeavor to search these matters along the path of the Scriptures and the tradition of the Fathers... Then gather the arguments so that . . . we may bring together what each of us has thought out by himself and decide then what we should write the Pope.[7]

Pope Nicholas had also written to Liutbert, Archbishop of Mainz,[8] with the same request. The result of the Carolingian effort was a work by Aeneas, Bishop of Paris, a work by Ratramnus, monk of Corbie, and a conciliar statement by the Council of Worms in 868.

On the issue of the procession of the Holy Spirit Pope Nicholas inadvertently misled the Carolingians. Although Pope Nicholas endorses the *doctrine* of the *Filioque,* he never refers to its interpolation in the Ecumenical Creed. Because of Pope Nicholas' endorsement of the *doctrine* of the *Filioque,* Ratramnus of Corbie simply assumes that Rome had added the *Filioque* to the Creed.

The Response of Aeneas of Paris

Aeneas responded with a work entitled *Liber adversus Graecos,*[9] a work which is simply a collection of patristic

---

[6]*PL* 126, 93-94.
[7]*PL* 126, 94.
[8]*MGH, Epistolae* VI, 610.
[9]*PL* 121, 683-721 (the triadological problem ends with column 721).

texts strikingly similar to the texts quoted in Theodulf's *De Spiritu Sancto*. Aeneas' introduction is the most interesting aspect of his work; it reveals the Carolingian attitude toward Byzantium, toward the See of Constantinople, and toward the Roman See. In words which could have been written by Photius he states:

> So the poisonous ruin of perverse dogma does not cease to creep about, gaining strength foully from the time of the origin of the Church until now, cleverly working to seize the incautious, to corrupt those quiet in dogma, to approach secretly like a thief those living good lives and to change truth to falsehood. But the Holy Church, as though worn by age, raises intercessory hands to heaven...[10]

Greece, writes Aenas, once the "mother of rhetoric and the fosterer of all liberal arts,"[11] has now attempted "to counsel even the Roman Church and every Latin-speaking nation."[12] Aeneas considers the questions in which the Greeks are engaged to be of "little worth," questions which have been "aired through long ages and clearly elucidated."[13] Greece, the "author of eloquence," is now the utterer of "dialectical subtility."[14]

Aeneas stresses that no one should be surprised that "such great and dangerous errors" have arisen from Constantinople, "for if the records of the Holy Canons and the ecclesiastical histories are examined, broods of vipers will be found to have arisen from those parts of the Empire...."[15] In contrast with the perfidious history of the

---

[10] *PL* 121, 685.

[11] *PL* 121, 686.

[12] *PL* 121, 686.

[13] *Ibid.*

[14] *Ibid.*

[15] *Ibid.*

See of Constantinople no heretic, claims Aeneas, has ever occupied the See of Rome.[16]

Aeneas, believing as most of the Carolingians that "the end of the world" is at hand, claims that this new attack by the Greeks on the Catholic Faith is a sign of the approaching end.

Following the same image evoked by Photius and Pope Nicholas, Aeneas also considers the controversy as a "war" and a "battlefield." "Let us believe," he writes, "that more are with us than with them; that is the very wise Fathers...."[17] The time of "holy combat" has come and the "true Israel" will now take vengeance on her enemies. For Aeneas, truth not only resides in the tradition preserved by the Roman See but also in the Latin language itself. "The Greek language should agree with the truth by which Latin indissolubly holds the norm of Catholic Faith."[18]

The "foolish stupidities" of the Greek accusations, writes Aeneas, have originated in an inexperienced intellect. But the "battleline of heavenly virtues"[19] will oppose these "foolish stupidities"; that is, "the defense of the illustrious Fathers, the agreement of the canons, and the victorious authority of very excellent bishops throughout the Christian world."[20] When the soldiers of Christ have finished this "war," when the battle is victorious, the "Father of the entire Church, the blessed Pontiff of the Apostolic See, will solemnly intone these words to God: 'But the Lord stood by me and gave me strength to proclaim the word fully, that all the Gentiles might hear it.'"[21]

---

[16]*PL* 121, 687. Aeneas is ostensibly unaware of the condemnation of Pope Honorius I (625-638) for monothelitism by the Sixth Ecumenical Council (Mansi 11, 622, 635, 655, and 666).

[17]*PL* 121, 688.

[18]*PL* 121, 689.

[19]*PL* 121, 690.

[20]*Ibid.*

[21]*PL* 121, 690; the quotation is from II Timothy 4:17.

Aeneas' first patristic authority is Athanasius, who occupied the See of Alexandria "which is second to the See of Rome."[22] All the quotations from Athanasius come from the pseudo-Athanasian corpus. Aeneas also quotes from the now traditional Latin sources. He quotes from Ambrose, Hilary, Cyril of Alexandria, Didymus-Jerome, Pope Hormisdas, Pope Leo, Pope Gregory, Fulgentius, Isidore, Prosper,[23] Vigilius of Thapsus, Proclus,[24] Agnellus, Cassiodorus and Prudentius.

The dominant patristic authority is again Augustine. Nineteen chapters of Aeneas' work are simply quotations from Augustine. He quotes from Augustine's *Tractatus in Joannis Evangelium, De Civitate Dei,*[25] *Contra Maximinum, De Incarnatione Domini,*[26] *Epistola* 178, and at great length from books I, III, VI and XV of Augustine's *De Trinitate*. One quotation ascribed to Augustine comes from the pseudo-Augustinian corpus.[27]

These patristic authorities are essentially the same as those adduced by the earlier Carolingian theologians in the first phase of the Triadological controversy. However,

---

[22]*PL* 121, 689. The Roman Church had never accepted the third canon of the Second Ecumenical Council and the twenty-eighth canon of the Fourth Ecumenical Council which gave the See of Constantinople second rank after the See of Rome and also conferred on Constantinople the title of "New Rome." This fact is constantly stressed by the Carolingian theologians; indeed it is even maintained that the See of Constantinople could not claim to be apostolic in the same sense that the Sees of Rome, Alexandria, Antioch and Jerusalem were apostolic.

[23]Actually, as in the case with Theodulf, this quotation is not from Prosper but from Julianus Pomerius' *De Vita contemplativa* 1, 18.

[24]As in the case with the quotation from Proclus by Theodulf, there is nothing in this quotation from Proclus by Aeneas which speaks of the procession of the Spirit from the Father and the Son. (*PL* 121, 717).

[25]*De Civitate Dei* 13, 24. The same text is quoted by Theodulf in *De Spiritu Sancto*.

[26]These quotations, as in the case with Theodulf, are not found in Augustine's *De Incarnatione Domini*.

[27]*PL* 121, 710.

with Aeneas' work a Carolingian theologian of the earlier period has now become an authority in his own right—Alcuin. Eleven chapters of Aeneas' work are quotations from Alcuin's *De Fide sanctae et individuae Trinitatis*.[28]

Aeneas also confirms the well-known fact that the Carolingians did not heed the request of Pope Leo III and continued using the interpolated Ecumenical Creed. Aeneas writes that the Catholic Faith which is sung by the entire Church of Gaul is: "I believe in the Holy Spirit . . . who proceeds from the Father and the Son."[29]

Aeneas' work shows no originality; it is merely a repetition of patristic texts. His use of Alcuin as an authoritative "Father" is noteworthy. Also of significance is the fact that he considers the West at "war" with the Greek East. Most important, however, is the fact that he considers the most important accusation of the Greeks to be the attack on the *Filioque*, the problem which he treats first in his work.

The Response of Ratramnus

The most ambitious and the most theologically significant work against the Greeks comes from the pen of Ratramnus of Corbie. In his *Contra Graecorum Opposita Romanam Ecclesiam infamantium*[30] Ratramnus does not merely appeal to Scripture and the Fathers; he theologizes on every text he quotes. It is most probable that Ratramnus' work, either in full or in part, reached Photius. Indeed, if no other work ever reached Photius, it was enough for him to have confronted a Greek translation or summary of Ratramnus' work for a full knowledge of Latin triadology.

---

[28]*PL* 121, 718-720.

[29]*PL* 121, 721; "qui ex Patre Filioque procedit."

[30]*PL* 121, 223-304 deal with the triadological problem.

It is significant that Ratramnus, as did Aeneas, considers the most important accusation of the Greeks to be the attack on the *Filioque*. Ratramnus' work, as that of Aeneas, directs its attack against the Greek Emperors specifically. The tone and spirit of the polemic is discernible at once. "The charges," writes Ratramnus, "with which the Greek Emperors, Basil and Michael, are trying to damage the Church of Rome are known to be false, heretical, superstitious and irreligious."[31] In fact, Ratramnus considers the charges "beneath contempt." The only reason a response is imperative is that the Greek accusations could bring harm "to the simple and the ignorant."[32] The key-note of Ratramnus' response is taken from Proverbs 26:5: "Respond to a fool according to his stupidity."[33] Quoting again from Proverbs, he warns the Greeks that "a false witness will not go unpunished."[34]

Following the statement of Pope Nicholas and agreeing with Aeneas, Ratramnus claims that the Greeks "strive to find fault not only with the Roman Church but with the entire Latin Church."[35] The specific reason for this attack against the entire West, writes Ratramnus, is that "we profess that the Holy Spirit proceeds from the Father and the Son, according to the Catholic Faith, while they claim the Spirit proceeds only from the Father."[36] The Greeks, therefore, depart from "communion with the Church" and "blaspheme against the Holy Spirit,"[37] the sin which is unpardonable.[38]

---

[31]*PL* 121, 225.

[32]*PL* 121, 226.

[33]*PL* 121, 227.

[34]*PL* 121, 227; Proverbs 19:5.

[35]*PL* 121, 227.

[36]*Ibid.*

[37]*Ibid.*

[38]*PL* 121, 272.

Ratramnus is certain that the tradition of the Church supports the Latins.

> When they say the Holy Spirit proceeds from the Father, they do not deny that he also proceeds from the Son. But if they wish to follow their Fathers, they will embrace the Catholic teaching that the Holy Spirit proceeds from the Father in the way their Fathers did, who, taught by sacred learning, well knew that he was the Spirit of both; that is, of the Father and of the Son as well.[39]

There is no Carolingian work which stresses the idea that since the Spirit is "of the Son," he must therefore proceed from the Son as much as Ratramnus'. Indeed, within every other argument Ratramnus also uses the theme of "the Spirit of the Son" and he eventually brings all these other arguments to this conclusion. The great stress on this theme in the work of Ratramnus is one of the reasons for suspecting that his work did reach Photius, for Photius dwells on this problem at great length in an attempt to prove that it does not follow that since the Spirit is the "Spirit of the Son," he therefore proceeds from the Son.

The Greek Emperors, writes Ratramnus, "laboring under the sickness of new doctrine or weakened by the virus of envy because they cannot be content with the boundaries of their Fathers," seek "to tear down the glory of their Fathers."[40]

In contrast with the innovations of the Greeks "no new cult is rising in the Roman Church, no new religion, no new doctrine, no new institution."[41]

> What our Fathers held and taught and left to posterity to cherish, this we hold and preserve, adding nothing, taking nothing away. What they taught about the Holy Spirit, that we believe. They received from the Apostles, and the Apostles from Christ. The Church both East and West has always remained in the same faith.[42]

---

[39] *PL* 121, 227.
[40] *PL* 121, 271.
[41] *PL* 121, 228.
[42] *PL* 121, 228; 244.

The Greek Emperors, writes Ratramnus, have usurped the power which belongs only to the Church. "Was it to the Greek Emperors that the Savior gave the power of binding and loosing?"[43] If the Greeks excommunicate the Roman Church, they would simply be excommunicating themselves from the Catholic Church. A prerequisite of being in the Church, writes Ratramnus, is being in communion with the See of Rome.

> If they think it enough that they know for certain that the Roman Church teaches that the Spirit proceeds from the Father and the Son, let them know that their Fathers also believed as the Romans believed. And while they want to deprive the Romans of communion, they at the same time excommunicate themselves from the company of their Fathers. *And none are in communion with the Catholic Church while they separate themselves from communion with Rome* . . . Let them quickly consider what an evil this act is and not delay in correcting their error, lest if they are unwilling to communicate with the Romans, they need to fear being excommunicated from the whole Catholic Church.[44]

Ratramnus' Appeal to Scripture

"You object," writes Ratramnus, "because we say the Holy Spirit proceeds from the Father and the Son. . . . Let us examine the Gospel . . . and take the tenor of our response from it."[45] Ratramnus begins at the heart of the matter. He quotes the Gospel of John which records Jesus as stating that the Spirit proceeds from the Father.[46] But the Greeks, argues Ratramnus, either do not read or else do not believe the Gospel when the Son also states that he shall send the Spirit from the Father. Either the Greeks must admit, claims Ratramnus, that this "sending is a procession," or fall into Arianism. Ratramnus wonders whether

---

[43] *PL* 121, 243.
[44] *PL* 121, 271-272.
[45] *PL* 121, 229.
[46] *PL* 121, 229; John 15:26.

the Greeks might be confused because the Son did not simply say "whom I shall send you" but added "from the Father." For Ratramnus, if one does not interpret the sending as a procession, then one makes "grades in the Divinity" and falls into Arianism.

Stressing the consubstantiality and inseparability of the Persons of the Trinity, Ratramnus maintains that the Spirit proceeds from the substance of the Father.

> The Holy Spirit proceeds from the Father because he flows from his substance. The Son sends the Spirit of Truth from the Father because, in order that the Holy Spirit proceed from the Son, the Son must be born from the Father. And just as the Son received his substance by birth from his Father, so likewise he receives from the Father that he might send the Spirit of Truth by proceeding from him. Moreover, when he says "who proceeds from the Father," he does not deny that the Holy Spirit proceeds from him because sending is of the Son, procession is of the Holy Spirit, so that he sends the Spirit of Truth not as though a greater in existence were sending a lesser by ordering; but by the word *sending*, it is shown that just as the Spirit of Truth proceeds from the Father, so he also proceeds from the Son . . . because just as the Father and the Son are of one substance, so too by procession from them both the Holy Spirit receives his consubstantial existence.[47]

When the Son states that "all that the Father has is mine,"[48] the Greeks most certainly, argues Ratramnus, should be able to discern the logical conclusions. "If the Son has whatever the Father has, surely just as the Holy Spirit is the Spirit of the Father, so he is also the Spirit of the Son."[49] If, argues Ratramnus, the Spirit proceeds only from the Father, then the Son does not have "all" that the Father has and the authority of Scripture cannot be relied on. But, maintains Ratramnus, Holy Scripture can be relied on; the Son does have "all" that the Father has and this includes the power which enables the Spirit to proceed from the Son

---

[47] *PL* 121, 229-230.
[48] John 16:15.
[49] *PL* 121, 230.

as well as from the Father because the Spirit is the Spirit of the Son.

> If you ask whence is the Spirit of Truth, ask also whence is the Spirit of the Father. Now he is the Spirit of the Father by proceeding from the Father. And likewise he is the Spirit of the Son by proceeding from the Son, who is Truth. This in no way implies subordination but signifies one and the same substance. For just as the Father and the Son are one and the same substance, so the Holy Spirit proceeds from the Father and the Son. You must not conclude that the Holy Spirit has two Fathers because he proceeds from the Father and the Son, since the Holy Spirit is not the Son, and he who is not a son cannot have a Father.

Concentrating on the Biblical statement that "God is love"[50] and following a line of thought from Augustine's *De Trinitate,* Ratramnus concludes that the Spirit proceeds from the Son.

> For with the love with which the Father loves the Son, with that same love the Son loves the Father. The love of the Father is the Holy Spirit and the Holy Spirit is also the love of the Son. The love of the Father proceeds from the Father to love the Son; the love of the Son proceeds from the Son to love the Father. Thus there is one love of them both because the one Spirit proceeds from both of them.[51]

From the texts in the New Testament which speak of "rivers of living water"[52] and a "spring of water"[53] Ratramnus concludes that the Spirit proceeds from the Son.

> The rivers of living water; that is, the Holy Spirit, proceed from Christ. For Christ is both perfect man and perfect God. As perfect God, he pours forth the Holy Spirit, who proceeds from him into those who believe in him.[54]

---

[50] I John 4:16.
[51] *PL* 121, 230-232.
[52] John 7:38-39.
[53] John 4:14.
[54] *PL* 121, 231.

From the fact that Christ breathed the Spirit on the disciples Ratramnus concludes that the Spirit must therefore proceed from the Son. "What does he signify by breathing if not the procession of the Holy Spirit?... He wanted to teach us by this that the Holy Spirit proceeds from himself and that the substance of the Holy Spirit flows from the substance of the Son."[55]

Taking Christ's statement that his words are "spirit and life,"[56] Ratramnus concludes from this that the Spirit proceeds from the Son. "Whence do words proceed but from the depths of the mind? Therefore, the words which he speaks are Spirit and life because the Spirit, who proceeds from the heart of Christ, is life."[57]

According to Ratramnus, Christ also testified that the Spirit proceeds from him when he exclaimed that "power" went forth from him.[58] "What is this expression . . . if not, 'I know there proceeds from me the Spirit'?"[59]

Ratramnus has a truly remarkable interpretation of the book of Revelation. He sees symbols of the Holy Spirit everywhere in this work and ultimately brings all his exegesis to the conclusion that the Spirit is the Spirit of the Son and hence proceeds from him. The "seven seals"[60] symbolize the "Holy Spirit because of the seven-fold grace he confers."[61]

> No Catholic, I think, will deny that the slain lamb is meant to be Christ . . . This lamb is said to have seven eyes, which signify the seven spirits of God. Not that there are seven persons . . . but they are called seven because of the seven-fold distribution of gifts . . . It is clear, therefore, that when he says the lamb has

---

[55] *PL* 121, 231.
[56] John 6:63; *PL* 121, 232.
[57] *PL* 121, 232.
[58] Luke 8:46.
[59] *PL* 121, 242.
[60] Revelation 5:5.
[61] *PL* 121, 237.

> seven eyes, he states that Christ *has* the Holy Spirit . . . who proceeds substantially from him.[62]
>
> Regard the golden candlestick as the incarnation of Christ . . . the light above his head is his divinity . . . the seven lamps on the candlestick or above his head are the fulness of the Holy Spirit . . . If the seven lights of the Holy Spirit rest on Christ, the Holy Spirit, who is symbolized by the seven lamps, also rests on him. And since he rests on him by dwelling in him substantially, he is the Spirit of the one on whom he rests substantially. Hence, he is rightly said to be the Spirit of Christ.[63]

Similarly, Ratramnus interprets the "white horse"[64] as the "body of Christ." The rider of the horse is the "divinity of Christ" and the eyes symbolize the Holy Spirit. "He shows by this image—indeed, he teaches very clearly, that the divinity of the Spirit proceeds from the divinity of the Son . . . so the Holy Spirit is the Spirit of Christ."[65]

In dealing with Biblical material, Ratramnus' main objective is to state those many texts which explicitly teach that the Spirit is the Spirit of the Son and to conclude from other texts that the Spirit is the Spirit of the Son. This is the essence of his Biblical methodology. If, therefore, the Spirit is the Spirit of the Son, he necessarily proceeds eternally *as existing* from the divine substance of the Father and the Son. "He cannot be 'of the substance of both' without proceeding from both."[66] "The Spirit proceeds from him, from whom he takes his substance . . . he, who is coupled in substance with the Father and the Son, *necessarily* proceeds from them both."[67]

> He receives his existence equally from the Father and the Son, as the Son receives his existence essentially from the Father. But the reverse is *not* true, that because the Holy Spirit proceeds equally

---

[62]PL 121, 238.
[63]PL 121, 239.
[64]Revelation 19.
[65]PL 121, 241-242.
[66]PL 121, 248.
[67]PL 121, 269.

from the Father and the Son, the Son too is born equally from the Father and the Holy Spirit. For birth is from the Father alone. Procession, however, is from both.[68]

Ratramnus' Appeal to the Ecumenical Councils

In appealing to the authority of the Ecumenical Councils, Ratramnus stresses the fact that the Council of Nicaea, the *First* Ecumenical Council, promulgated an Ecumenical Creed which simply stated in reference to the Holy Spirit: "We believe in the Holy Spirit."[69] He underscores the fact that the Second Ecumenical Council *added* to that original Ecumenical Creed by stating that the Holy Spirit "proceeds from the Father...." "Did it deny," asks Ratramnus, "that the Holy Spirit proceeds from the Son? Or does it follow that if he proceeds from the Father, he does not proceed from the Son?"[70] To assure the Greeks that the Council did not *deny* the procession of the Spirit from the Son, Ratramnus again repeats Augustine's dialectic of love.

> No one can deny that the Holy Spirit proceeds from the Son unless he denies that the Son has the love with which he loves the Father . . . it must be held and faithfully professed that the Father loves the Son and the Son loves the Father. And this love with which the Father loves the Son proceeds from the Father and the love with which the Son loves the Father proceeds from the Son. This love is the Holy Spirit.[71]

Ratramnus argues that if the Council of Constantinople had the *right* to add to the original Ecumenical Creed, then "this same *right* was given to the Romans through the authority of Holy Scripture."[72] Ratramnus' position, brought out very clearly in his defense of Roman primacy in the

---

[68]*PL* 121, 240.
[69]*PL* 121, 245.
[70]*PL* 121, 243-244.
[71]*PL* 121, 243.
[72]*PL* 121, 245.

latter part of his work, is that Christ gave the supreme primacy and authority of the Church to the Bishop of Rome. Hence, the Bishop of Rome certainly has the *same right* which an Ecumenical Council has. "You cannot prove that the city of Constantinople has greater authority than Rome, which is the head of all the churches of Christ."[73]

Ratramnus, using the *theology of interpolation* developed earlier by Paulinus of Aquileia, argues that the Second Ecumenical Council set the precedent for adding to the Ecumenical Creed. Ratramnus accepts essentially the two criteria established by Paulinus for "legitimately" adding to the Creed. Any addition to the Ecumenical Creed must be in harmony with the meaning of Scripture and its objective must be to combat heresy.[74] If the Second Ecumenical Council could *add* to the Creed, then the Greeks, argues Ratramnus, must "grant to the Latin Churches the same right . . . that, although the Gospels do not state in exact words that the Holy proceeds from the Son, yet they show in many ways that he is the Spirit of the Son just as he is the Spirit of the Father and proceeds from the Son just as he proceeds from the Father."[75]

Ratramnus proposes a most unusual solution of the problem. If the Greeks remove the statement from the Creed which was *added* by the Council of Constantinople, then "perhaps what was *added* by the Roman Church may be removed."[76] In fact, however, the Roman Church had not added to the Creed.

Ratramnus maintains that the *Filioque* is the only way to distinguish between the eternal "begetting" of the Son and the eternal "procession" of the Spirit. If the Greeks think that the introduction of the word "procession" to the

---

[73]*Ibid.*

[74]*Ibid.* Paulinus is more explicit, claiming that any addition to the Creed must not contradict the intention of the *Fathers.*

[75]*PL* 121, 245.

[76]*Ibid.*

Creed safeguarded the distinction between the person of the Son and the person of the Spirit, they are quite mistaken. "Know that the word procession is also used of the Son."⁷⁷ Ratramnus' reference is to John 8:42 which in the Latin text of the New Testament uses the word *procession* in relation to the Son.⁷⁸ Since, according to Ratramnus, the New Testament uses the word *procession* in relation to the Son and since the Second Ecumenical Council used the word *procession* in relation to the Spirit, the only way to distinguish the "procession" of the Son and the "procession" of the Spirit is by means of the *Filioque*. With the *Filioque* there is a guarantee that no one will confuse the procession of the Son and the procession of the Spirit, for the Son "proceeds" only from the Father while the Spirit proceeds from both. If there is not this safeguard, Ratramnus asks "what will impose silence on the Arians to prevent them from blasphemously saying that the Holy Spirit is the Son the Father?"⁷⁹

Ratramnus' Appeal to the Fathers

Ratramnus is convinced that both the Latin and the Greek Fathers taught that the Spirit proceeds from the Father and the Son. "Both Latin and Greek Fathers," writes Ratramnus, "examined this question and said that the Son alone is born of the Father, but the Holy Spirit proceeds from the Father and the Son."⁸⁰ Again, his basic position is that the "Fathers knew he was the Spirit of both the Father and the Son and therefore proceeds from both."⁸¹

---

⁷⁷*PL* 121, 247.

⁷⁸*Ibid*. The Latin text is: "Ego ex Deo *processi* et veni..." The word in the original Greek is not one of the later patristic equivalents of procession: "ἐγὼ γὰρ ἐκ τοῦ Θεοῦ ἐξῆλθον καὶ ἥκω..."

⁷⁹*PL* 121, 247.

⁸⁰*PL* 121, 247.

⁸¹*PL* 121, 247.

Ratramnus appeals to the Athanasian Creed, quoting it in good faith as the work of Athanasius. "The Latin doctors," he writes, approved the doctrine of Athanasius and later added "who proceeds from the Father and the Son" to the Creed to combat the heresy of Arianism.[82]

It is significant that Ratramnus begins his quite lengthy treatment of texts from Gregory of Nazianzus with an introductory challenge: "Tell us whether you profess that the Holy Spirit is the Spirit of Christ?"[83] And that is precisely where Ratramnus brings every statement of Gregory of Nazianzus; that is, to the conclusion that Gregory believed that the Spirit is the Spirit of the Son. Ratramnus' conclusion, of course, is that since Gregory believed the Spirit is of the Son, then he must have believed that the Spirit proceeds from the Son, a conclusion which Gregory never arrived at. Ratramnus also maintains that Gregory's teaching of the consubstantiality of the Father, Son, and Holy Spirit implies a procession of the Spirit from the Son.

> From that time until now more than 500 years have elapsed and never has the procession of the Holy Spirit from the Son been denied. No question concerning it arose among Catholics except only in our own times. The professions of faith of the Church both East and West about the Holy Spirit remained one and the same.[84]

Ratramnus also appeals to the authority of Ambrose, Didymus, Paschasius, Pope Gregory, Gennadius and Fulgentius, stressing the fact that none of these authorities was ever "out of favor with or considered heretical by" the Greek Emperors of those days. "For the Emperors of the time who reigned not only at Constantinople but also at Rome knew that the dogma was Catholic and the faith Apostolic."[85] These Fathers testify that the Church was never divided on this

---

[82]*PL* 121, 247.
[83]*PL* 121, 248.
[84]*PL* 121, 253.
[85]*PL* 121, 266.

issue and that it never "thought or taught differently about the Holy Spirit."[86]

But the most important patristic authority for Ratramnus is "Father Augustine, distinguished Doctor and most outstanding among Church leaders."[87] Ratramnus anticipates a possible Greek reply concerning Augustine. "Perhaps the pride of the Greeks will oppose this, claiming that they are unwilling to receive the authority of the Latins."[88] If the Greeks are not willing to accept the authority of Augustine or other Latins, then they refuse, writes Ratramnus, to accept the very principle of the "ecumenicity" of the Church.[89] "If you do not want to listen to Augustine, listen to Christ and the Apostle."[90]

No Carolingian theologian so thoroughly mastered the triadological thought of Augustine as Ratramnus. He does not simply quote from Augustine; he explains and interprets at length each Augustinian text he quotes. His interpretation of Augustine, which takes up twenty-three columns in Migne, deals with almost every aspect of Augustinian triadology.

Ratramnus' work is the most impressive one of the Carolingian theologians on this problem. Ratramnus was indeed a prisoner of history. He was unaware that the *Filioque* had not been used as yet in the Ecumenical Creed at Rome, but the tenor of Pope Nicholas' position certainly led him to think that the papacy not only supported the doctrine of the *Filioque* but also supported its interpolation in the Creed. He was unaware that the controversy over the procession of the Holy Spirit had in fact occurred in the past. And he faced the hermeneutical problem of reading the texts of the Greek Fathers from within the perspective of the Latin

---

[86]*PL* 121, 270.
[87]*PL* 121, 271.
[88]*PL* 121, 272.
[89]*PL* 121, 272.
[90]*PL* 121, 274.

model of the Holy Trinity. Aside from this historical conditioning, everything else in Ratramnus' work follows quite logically. Even his approach to the authority of the Ecumenical Councils has an implicit logic behind it which avoids the dangerous tendency in Paulinus of Aquileia's *theology of interpolation*. Ratramnus, concluding from the nature of Pope Nicholas' letter that Rome had *added* the *Filioque* to the Ecumenical Creed, easily supports the legitimacy of the *Filioque* addition by means of his view of the primacy of the Roman See. According to Ratramnus, the Bishop of Rome, by the power given him through St. Peter, is equal to or superior to an Ecumenical Council. What an Ecumenical Council might have the *right* to do, the Bishop of Rome certainly had the *right* to do. Thus there was a certain inner logic in Ratramnus' approach to the problem.

The Response of the Council of Worms

The German Bishops at the Council of Worms in 868 issued a conciliar statement against the Greeks.[91] There is only one thing noteworthy about this conciliar statement concerning the triadological problem. The Council claimed that it would be swept too far if it collected all the texts from the Fathers which strike down the "barbaric and ludicrous" charges of the Greek Emperors. The Council concluded that it was enough to oppose only one Father to the Greeks and that Father is Augustine. Five columns of quotations from Doctor Augustine then follow on the subject of the procession of the Spirit or, which was the same for the Carolingians, the Spirit's consubstantiality with the Father and the Son. In quoting from Augustine, it is noteworthy that there are no quotations from *De Trinitate*.[92]

---

[91]*PL* 119, 1201-1212; *Responsio Episcoporum Germaniae Wormatiae coadunatorum De Fide Sanctae Trinitatis*. Only the first five columns deal with problem of the *Filioque*.

[92]The Council quotes only from Augustine's Sermons, his Letters, his Commentary on John and Matthew, and his *De Civitate Dei*.

The Latin Response to Photius' Encyclical

The Acts of the Council of Worms were signed by many Archbishops, Bishops, and Abbots.[93] Pope Nicholas' request had been carried out. Precisely what ultimately reached Photius is unknown. But it is quite possible that all these works may have reached Constantinople, along with some works which may have been written in Rome.

In 867 Pope Nicholas died and Photius was deposed. Photius, however, had not had his final say.

---

[93] The Acts of this council were signed by Archbishops Adalwinus, Liutbus, Rimbtus; by Bishops Anno, Salomon, Gunzo, Arno, Witgarius, Luitbus, Ambrico, Otgarius, Gebehardus, Ratolfus, Ermricus, Hessi, Hildegrimus, Theodricus, Egibertus, Erolfus, Luithardus, Lantfridus; and by Abbots Theoto, Adalgarius, Hetto, Brunwardus, Aschericus, Theotrocus, and Egilbertus.

CHAPTER IX

The Photian Council of 879-880

Byzantine Internal Problems

In 867 there was a new Emperor in Byzantium, Emperor Basil I (867-886), who initiated a pro-Roman See policy perhaps, as Dvornik suggests, "to screen his murder behind the authority" of the Roman See.[1] A necessary step in moving toward better relations with the Roman See was the removal of Photius as Patriarch. The evidence[2] seems to support the position that Photius submitted his resignation and that Ignatius was again (867-878) installed as Patriarch. Pope Hadrian II (867-872) demanded that the acts of the Photian Council of 867, convoked as a result of Photius' Encyclical to the Eastern Patriarchs, be burned in Constantinople as they had been burned in Rome. Papal legates, upon arriving in Constantinople, informed Emperor Basil that no one would

---

[1]Francis Dvornik, *The Photian Schism* (Cambridge: University Press, 1948), p. 143.

[2]See Dvornik, *op. cit.*, p. 136 f.

be admitted to the new council unless he first signed a "long and vehement condemnation of Photius."³ Basil was forced, as a result of his new policy, to concede and the Council opened on October 5, 869.⁴

To prevent the utter humiliation of the Byzantines, Emperor Basil disregarded two papal orders: he refused to allow the papal legates to preside and demanded that Photius be given a hearing. Photius, however, remained silent and, refusing to sign his own condemnation, was excommunicated by the papal legates.

While the Council was in session a Bulgarian embassy arrived in Constantinople to determine to which Patriarchate Bulgaria belonged. Emperor Basil at once called a conference attended by the legates of the Eastern Patriarchs and the Bulgarian envoys, but not the papal legates. The Eastern Patriarchs declared that Bulgaria belonged to the Patriarchate of Constantinople.⁵ The papal legates produced a letter from Pope Hadrian which forbade Ignatius from interfering in Bulgaria. The evidence seems to support the position that the Roman See approved Ignatius only on condition that he keep Byzantine missionaries out of Bulgaria.⁶

Photius was exiled and at first treated rather harshly. His greatest hardship, he wrote, was not having access to his library. Patriarch Ignatius had problems in his second term as Patriarch because he did not represent the main-

---

³*Ibid.*, p. 145.

⁴Dvornik writes that the papal legates "must have been painfully surprised" when only twelve bishops attended the first session. After nine sessions the papal legates had obtained only 103 signatures, which surprised even Anastasius Bibliothecarius (Mansi 16, 45).

⁵Dvornik writes that "the decision was not as unfair to Rome as the legates pretended. Canonically, the Byzantine claim was legitimate, since Bulgaria included only a small portion of Macedonia which had been under Roman jurisdiction and included a great part of Thrace which had always been under the jurisdiction of Constantinople."

⁶Pope John VIII's letter to Michael-Boris of Bulgaria would confirm this. See *MGH, Epistolae* VII, p. 294 and Dvornik, *op. cit.*, p. 156 for a partial English translation.

stream of the Byzantine clergy. Emperor Basil gradually softened the condition of the exiled Photius, finally allowing him to return to the imperial palace. The Emperor entrusted the education of his son, the future Emperor Leo VI (886-912), to Photius.

When Ignatius died in 878, Photius again became Patriarch (878-886). Pope John VIII (872-882) accepted Photius as Patriarch with the stipulation that Photius apologize before a council for his former actions, refrain from interfering with Roman missionary activity in Bulgaria, and never again allow a layman to rise to the episcopacy without proper regulation. Pope John VIII ordered all the Ignatian clergy to recognize Photius as the legitimate Patriarch or else face excommunication.

The Council of 879-880

Pope John VIII acceded to Emperor Basil's request for another council. Pope John sent Patriarch Photius a letter which stressed that the papal legates had special instructions contained in a *Commonitorium*. This *Commonitorium*, the Latin text of which is not extant, was read at the fourth session of the Council of 879-880. Because the tenth clause[7] ordered the suppression of the anti-Photian council, which later became the Eighth Ecumenical Council for the Latin West, the Commonitorium was long considered a forgery. The research of Dvornik has now altered that view.[8] "What

---

[7] Mansi 17, 472.

[8] The last letter of Pope John to the Ignatians warns them not to "find excuses in writings on the subject, since all fetters are unfastened by the divine power which the Church of Christ has received, whenever what is bound is undone by our pastoral authority." (Quoted from Dvornik, *op. cit.,* p. 175f.). Dvornik concludes that "it is evident that the Pope refers here to the Acts of the Eighth Council.... Therefore, even the fetters that bound Photius were undone. How then could fetters that were undone

in my opinion," writes Dvornik, "enhances the historical value of this document and corroborates its authority is the fact that other instructions given to the legates correspond nearly word for word with certain passages of the pontifical letters."[9]

The sixth session of the Council of 879-880 has enormous bearing on the Triadological controversy. This session, as well as the seventh session, was also once considered a forgery, a view which finds little acceptance today.[10] One of the reasons for doubting the authenticity of these sessions was that the sixth session, unlike the previous sessions, met in the Imperial palace. There was, however, a most important reason for this. The Emperor had been unable to attend any of the previous sessions because he was in mourning for his dead son. Without the Emperor's signature the decisions of the Council could not become law in the Empire. Hence, the sixth session took place in the Imperial palace to conform with the rules of Byzantine etiquette. Out of respect for the Emperor only Photius, the papal legates, and eighteen metropolitans and archbishops attended the sixth session.

At the sixth session of this Council Photius finally accomplished what he had long sought. The papal legates signed a carefully worded statement by Photius on the prohibition of any alteration of the Nicene-Constantinopolitan Creed.

> Firmly grounded in the venerable and divine doctrine of our Lord and Savior Jesus Christ, with unquestioned determination

---

keep the force of law that was revoked by supreme authority? The Roman synods of 863 and 869 as well as the Council of 869-870 were summoned solely against Photius and the Patriarch's condemnation was virtually the only topic of their deliberations: if these decisions are declared to be valueless, what is left of the synods?" (Dvornik, *op. cit.*, p. 177).

[9]Dvornik, *op. cit.*, p. 178.

[10]Hergenröther accepts the authenticity of these sessions (*op. cit.*, II, pp. 528-540). See also Amann, *op. cit.*, pp. 465 and 490f. Even Martin Jugie accepts the authenticity of these sessions. See "Schisme" in *Dictionnaire de Théologie Catholique* (1939), XIV, 1340ff.

and with full purity of faith in deep reverence and loyal preservation of the Holy precepts of his disciples and apostles, and in complete fidelity to the errorless canonical laws and the immutable faith of the doctrine and canons of the Seven Holy and Ecumenical Councils, which were inspired and guided by one and the same Holy Spirit, we reject those who separate themselves from the Church and we embrace and receive those who are worthy of reception, those who are of the same mind...

This we think and teach—that we accept with both heart and mouth the Creed of Faith which was transmitted from of old by the Fathers up to this very time. And we all proclaim with a loud voice that this Creed cannot be subtracted from, added to, altered or distorted in any way...

This Holy and *Ecumenical* Council accepts with complete divine zeal and total purity of intention the ancient Creed of Faith.... And [this Council] glorifies it and establishes the confidence of salvation upon it and declares it aloud so that all can therefore learn it.[11]

The Nicene-Constantinopolitan Creed, without the *Filioque* interpolation, then follows. The Council then declared that no one could put forward another Creed, that no one could add "unauthentic or falsified expressions" to this ancient Creed. Anyone attempting to deform the "most Holy and Venerable Creed" in any way was to be excommunicated. The Council then declared that if anyone "thinks otherwise, he will be considered an enemy of God and of Truth."

There is no doubt that the papal legates, Paul, Eugenius and Cardinal Peter, signed the conciliar statement. It is also quite clear, especially from Photius' later writings,[12] that Photius had hoped the signatures of the Roman legates to the decisions of this "Ecumenical" Conciliar decision would put an end to the use of the interpolated Creed in the Western provinces under the Roman Patriarch. If the See

---

[11]Mansi 17, 516. The above text was translated into English from Hergenröther's German translation because Hergenröther maintains that the text in Mansi is not complete. See Hergenröther, *op. cit.,* II, 518f.

[12]See Photius' letter to the Patriarch of Aquileia (*PG* 102, 820) and Photius' *Mystagogia* (*PG* 102, 380).

of Rome, the Patriarchate of the West and the See holding the primacy in the Church, committed itself to an uninterpolated Creed, then Photius could, he thought, rest assured that the ultimate victory over the interpolated *Filioque* had been won. Had not a similar situation arisen with the decisions of the Seventh Ecumenical Council? Had not the Franks opposed these decisions also? And did not the position of the Roman See ultimately triumph?

Pope John's Letter to Photius

Dvornik's traditionally precise scholarship tends to lapse when he cursorily considers the subject of the authenticity of Pope John's letter to Photius. Unfortunately, Dvornik has not really given serious consideration to the authenticity of this letter; he has simply, and admittedly, taken the conclusion of Hergenröther for granted. "Hergenröther," writes Dvornik, "came to the conclusion that the document was a forgery . . . In agreement with Hergenröther's finding, I have placed the forgery in the fourteenth century and know of no reason for revising this conclusion."[13] Later, however, Dvornik modifies his earlier statement. He writes that "on the whole, it is not absolutely impossible, but most unlikely, that John VIII should have written to Photius on the addition to the Symbol...."[14] Furthermore, it is noteworthy that Dvornik disagrees with Hergenröther's specific conclusion that the alleged letter of Pope John touches on the *doctrine* of the *Filioque*. "All that the author is concerned with," writes Dvornik, "is the addition of the *Filioque* to the Symbol."[15]

---

[13]Dvornik, *op. cit.*, p. 197.

[14]*Ibid.*, p. 198.

[15]*Ibid.*

Dvornik's knowledge of the Triadological controversy is ostensibly incomplete. If he had better knowledge of the history of the controversy, his conclusions might have been different.

There was every reason why Pope John VIII should have written Photius on this issue. In the letter allegedly written by Pope John the Pope states that Photius had sent legates to Rome to discuss the issue. It is known from Photius' later writings that papal legates came three times to Constantinople to discuss the matter. Pope John also had before him the "silver shields" erected by Pope Leo III as a constant reminder. And there is no evidence that Rome itself had added the interpolated *Filioque* to the Creed in Rome. What is remarkable about this letter is that Pope John's position is the same as that of Pope Leo III. This letter, which Mansi published at the end of the Acts of the Council of 879-880,[16] concurs with all other historical evidence, with Photius' later remarks about his beloved Pope John, and the letter has the "ring of truth" to it.

> We are aware of the negative reports you have heard about us and our Church. Therefore, I seek to explain myself to you before you write to me on the subject. You are aware that your envoy discussed the issue of the Creed with us and that he found we preserve it as we originally received it without adding anything or taking anything from it. For we know that anyone who tampers with it deserves punishment. We assure you, therefore, concerning this issue which has been a scandal to the Church, that we not only recite it [in the original version] but even condemn those foolish ones who have had the presumption to act otherwise . . . as violators of the divine words and distorters of the teachings of Christ the Lord . . . and of the Fathers who transmitted the Holy Creed to us through the Councils. We judge them with Judas because they have done as he did, since, although it is not the Body of Christ which they subject to death, they nevertheless bring schism to the faithful who are his members. . .
>
> But, I think your wise Holiness well knows how difficult it is to change immediately a custom which has been entrenched for so many years. Therefore, we believe the best policy is not to force anyone to abandon that addition to the Creed. But rather we must

---

[16] Mansi 17, 523 and 526.

act with wisdom and moderation, urging them little by little to give up that blasphemy. Therefore, those who claim we share this opinion are not correct. Those, however, who claim that there are those among us who dare to recite the Creed in this way are correct.
Your Holiness must not be scandalized because of this nor withdraw from the sound part of the body of our Church. Rather, you should aid us energetically with gentleness and wisdom in attempting to convert those who have departed from the truth...[17]

What supports the authenticity of this letter is precisely Pope John's way of handling Photius and the advice he gives to Photius. Who in the fourteenth century would have been concerned with the details given by Pope John? If it had been a Byzantine forgery, Pope John's strategy would indeed appear strange. It would appear that Photius understood quite well the policy of the Roman See. Although the Roman See itself would not alter the Creed, it had nevertheless committed itself to a policy of inaction. Photius, from the tone and content of his later writings, realized that the "war" against some within the Roman Patriarchate; namely, the Franks, had not ended. Photius apparently realized that the decisions of the Council of 879-880 were not as easily enforceable as were the decisions of the Seventh Ecumenical Council.

---

[17]Mansi 17, 523 and 526.

CHAPTER X

Photius' Letter to the Patriarch of Aquileia

Photius' letter to the Patriarch of Aquileia[1] was written between 883 and 884.[2] Hergenröther speculated that Photius knew of the Acts of the Council of Friuli under Patriarch Paulinus and hence wrote the letter in an attempt to extirpate the interpolated *Filioque* from the very place where a *theology of interpolation* was worked out. This letter is also consistent with the policy of Pope John; that is, to handle the situation energetically but wisely. From the content of the letter it is clear that Photius had received the Carolingian works.[3]

---

[1] *PG* 102, 794-822.

[2] There is much uncertainty about identifying the person who received this letter. Under Pope John VIII and his successors there were two rival groups contending for the title of "Patriarch of Aquileia." One group was at Aquileia under Walpert; the other at Grado under Palladius. The letter could have been written to either of them.

[3] Hergenröther claims he discerns evidence in this letter that Photius did have Ratramnus' work. See Hergenröther, *op. cit.*, II, 642f.

After rhetorically praising the virtues of the Patriarch of Aquileia, Photius arrives at the heart of the matter.

> But while this opinion of your holy virtue had come to us and we were glorifying and rejoicing.... What now falls on our ears (and would that it never had, for it is a great sadness ... therefore we considered it worthwhile to lay open this sorrow...). I do not know how I can speak of it without a bitter and saddened spirit. For just as though the words of the Lord were not good or sufficient for them, or as if they had no regard for the Councils and definitions and decrees of the Fathers, and spurn their diligence in their name or have blind minds in such matters, I know not how anyone can even speak of it—it has come to our ears (would that it were not so)—that some in the West are introducing as a new teaching the statement that the Divine and Most Holy Spirit proceeds not from God the Father but also from the Son.[4]

Photius writes that after "investigation" of the matter, it was concluded that their position contradicts "not only ... texts in Holy Scripture but also ... the words of the Lord."[5] Unless they "come quickly back to their senses from an absurd opinion," they open themselves to great blasphemy and condemnation and will depart "from the Divine Spirit himself."[6]

Photius appeals to the testimony of the Roman Popes. He writes that Pope Leo the Great, in accepting the Fourth Ecumenical Council, "declared that the Holy Spirit proceeds from the Father, according to the previous decrees, but not from the Son."[7] Photius refers to Pope Leo III as the "younger Leo," who, "in order to preserve the pure Creed from corruption in any way by barbarous language, declared that the Divine and Holy Trinity should be praised and preached in Greek to those in the West, as it had been decreed and read from the beginning."[8] "He also inscribed it," writes Photius, "on certain shields, like inscriptions on columns,

---

[4]*PG* 102, 797.
[5]*PG* 102, 797.
[6]*PG* 102, 797.
[7]*PG* 102, 800.
[8]*PG* 102, 800.

and placed it before the eyes of all and affixed it to the doors of the Church."⁹ Photius' account of Pope Leo's action is not, of course, thoroughly accurate. Only one shield was engraved in Greek. No Roman Bishop would have maintained that Greek should in any way be the ecclesiastical language of the Latin West.

Photius also refers to Hadrian I (772-795) "who ruled the same Apostolic See . . . [and] wrote to the most holy and blessed Tarasius," maintaining "clearly" that the "Holy Spirit proceeds from the Father and not from the Son."¹⁰

Photius firmly believes that the Roman Church, "together with the other four major Sees of the priesthood,"¹¹ professes the same. "Whence and from whom," asks Photius, "has this new blasphemy against the Spirit emerged?"¹² He states that "much diligence is needed to restrain the progress of this evil...."¹³ He calls upon the Patriarch of Aquileia to lead his flock "away from error and lead them by the hand" back to the original "piety" of the Christian Church.¹⁴

In his theological explication of the doctrine of the procession of the Holy Spirit Photius first of all maintains that the words of the Lord support the doctrine that the Spirit proceeds from the Father.¹⁵

> If they raised their eyes at any time to this torch, those who blasphemously teach the procession of the Spirit from the Son would cease to be in error and darkness. Illumined by the light of faith, they would enter the fold in equal covenant with the Orthodox, radiating the light of Orthodoxy which knows no setting. Reverencing especially him who drank in from the Lord's breast and was made disciple and teacher of heavenly dogmas and received the name of John the Theologian,

---

[9] *PG* 102, 800.
[10] *PG* 102, 817.
[11] *PG* 102, 800.
[12] *PG* 102, 801.
[13] *PG* 102, 801.
[14] *PG* 102, 801.
[15] *PG* 102, 801.

they would pray for pardon through his intercession for having ever opposed him and his teaching by contrary opinions...[16]

Photius explains to the Patriarch of Aquileia that if the Spirit proceeds from the Father and the Son, then one "introduces two causes and origins and utterly destroys the monarchy in the Holy Trinity."[17]

Repeating his earlier argument contained in his Encyclical, Photius argues that "if the procession from the Father is perfect, what need is there of another procession . . . if it is imperfect, who will tolerate such an absurd assertion?"[18]

Admitting that he knows the proponents of the *Filioque* do not consider the Spirit a grandson, nevertheless, contends Photius, the idea is implicit in their teaching. "For if the Son comes from the Father by generation and the Spirit comes from the Son by procession, clearly he enters the rank of grandson."[19]

Photius develops a new argument centered around the idea of the "eternal" nature of the "begetting of the Son" and the "procession of the Spirit."

> If the Spirit proceeds from the Son, he will proceed not later and not earlier than the begetting of the Son, for . . . time . . . [is] totally eliminated from the Most Holy Trinity. If then the Spirit proceeds at the same time from the Father and the Son, he will be distinct from the two producing Persons. And, instead of being one [Spirit], he will be a double Spirit . . . one who proceeds from the Father and another who proceeds from the Son.[20]

Photius develops this idea further. In the eternality of the Godhead, the Spirit must proceed from the Son at the same "time" that the Son is begotten. According to the logics of the *Filioque* doctrine, Photius claims that "the Spirit as

---

[16] *PG* 102, 801.
[17] *PG* 102, 801.
[18] *PG* 102, 801.
[19] *PG* 102, 804.
[20] *PG* 102, 806.

well as the Son will proceed from the Father by begetting."[21] Logically, the advocates of the *Filioque* doctrine, argues Photius, must declare that the Spirit "is later than the generation of the Son and younger than the Son."[22]

Photius, obviously referring to the Carolingian works he had received, states: "I hear they dare to charge Paul . . . as the author of this heresy. . . ."[23] Photius utilizes the texts quoted by the Carolingians which state that since the Spirit is the Spirit of the Son, he must proceed from the Son. Photius accuses them of distorting the texts of Scripture.

> Paul . . . said the Spirit was sent by the Father. Say the same thing Paul said! For he is the Spirit of the Son . . . He did not say he proceeds from the Son . . . But if they think that because he is called the Spirit of the Son, he therefore proceeds [from the Son], then they will also teach that the Father proceeds from the Son, for the Father is everywhere called [the Father] of the Son.[24]

Photius brings the Latin interpretation of these texts *ad absurdum* by stating that the Spirit is also called the Spirit of "wisdom, knowledge, understanding and fortitude" and yet he does not proceed from these,[25] an idea he will develop at greater length in his *Mystagogia*.

Photius takes another Carolingian interpretation and attempts to show that it proves exactly the opposite of what they contend. "For they say the Savior said 'He will take what is mine and announce it to you'."[26] But Photius asks "what is more obvious for proving that the Spirit proceeds not from the Son but from the Father?"[27] In his *Mystagogia* Photius develops this idea, pointing out that the Son does not say "of me" but rather "of mine"; that is, of that which

---

[21]*PG* 102, 804.
[22]*PG* 102, 804.
[23]*PG* 102, 804.
[24]*PG* 102, 804 and 806.
[25]*PG* 102, 804 and 806.
[26]*PG* 102, 808.
[27]*PG* 102, 808.

he received from the Father. Even if the text stated that "he will receive of me" and not "of that which is mine,"[28] they would be able to prove nothing, claims Photius, "for to receive does not always have the same meaning as to proceed.... For it is one thing to receive and drink in one substance from another substance, and another thing to proceed as (an existing) substance and person."[29]

Photius is now aware that the Carolingians appeal to Augustine and other Latin Fathers "who have written in many places . . . that the Holy Spirit proceeds from the Son."[30] Photius had apparently confronted the Carolingian works or Greek summaries of them, for he writes: "we are indeed persuaded that they thought this."[31] Photius' way of handling their appeal to the Latin Fathers is most noteworthy. He first warns that one must be careful in handling the texts of the "Fathers." "If ten or twenty Fathers said this, many innumerable hundreds did not."[32] According to Photius, one cannot restrict oneself to a handful of Fathers who contradict the decisions of the Ecumenical Councils. Secondly, Photius claims that by appealing to these Latin Fathers in support of heresy, the Carolingians are actually "uncovering" the errors of these good men. The proper act of respect for these venerable Fathers, who erred on this one issue, would be to conceal their weakness rather than acting in imitation of Ham, another idea which Photius develops more fully in his *Mystagogia*.[33] And, thirdly, the ones who harm "holy Augustine" and other Latin Fathers are those who oppose their teaching to the teaching of Christ and the teaching of the Ecumenical Councils. "If the Fathers . . . did not speak against our Lord, we too will not speak against them. But

---

[28]*PG* 102, 808. "'Εξ ἐμοῦ, ἀλλ' ἐκ τοῦ ἐμοῦ."
[29]*PG* 102, 809.
[30]*PG* 102, 809.
[31]*PG* 102, 809.
[32]*PG* 102, 809.
[33]*PG* 102, 811.

if you say they opposed the word of the Lord, it is your duty to prefer the word of the Lord to them...."[34]

Photius maintains that one should sympathize with these Fathers because they lived in time of great perplexity and many historical influences may have led them to false teaching on a few issues.

> If [these] ... Fathers had spoken in opposition when the debated question was brought before them and had fought it contentiously and had maintained their opinion and had persevered in this false teaching, and when convicted of it had held to their doctrine until death, then they would necessarily be rejected together with the error of their mind. But if they spoke badly or, for some reason not known to us, deviated from the right path, but no question was put to them nor did anyone challenge them to learn the truth, we admit them to the list of Fathers, as if they had not said it—because of their righteousness of life and distinguished virtue and their faith, faultless in other respects. We do not, however, follow their teaching in which they stray from the path of truth ... We, though, who know that some of our Holy Fathers and teachers strayed from the faith of true dogmas, do not take as doctrine those areas in which they strayed, but we embrace the men. So also in the case of any who are charged with teaching that the Spirit proceeds from the Son, we do not admit what is opposed to the word of the Lord, but we do not cast them from the rank of the Fathers.[35]

Photius has a lucidly liberal and fair theology of what constitutes a "Father." Augustine retains the rank of "Father," even though he erred on certain issues. Photius obviously does not accept the position, used by the Fifth Ecumenical Council, that one can judge a Father after death. "Since one who is dead is present neither through himself nor through others who would undertake his defense, no one of sound mind would wish to contend against him."[36]

Photius argues that "not even if *all* creatures had a single voice"; that is, expressing the *Filioque,* "would anyone

---

[34]*PG* 102, 811.
[35]*PG* 102, 813.
[36]*PG* 102, 816.

pay attention to creatures speaking against the Creator."[37] If the Patriarch of Aquileia wants to appeal to an authority, "then look first to Christ himself." Then one should look to the authority of the Ecumenical Councils. Look also, exhorts Photius, to the position taken by the Roman Popes. Photius calls the attention of the Patriarch of Aquileia to the recent acts of the sixth session of the Council of 879-880.

> This also . . . I ought not to omit, even though all are aware of it because it took place so recently. The legates from Old Rome who recently came to us not once but even three times to discuss with us [this matter] of faith . . . neither said nor were found to hold anything different or opposed to the faith which was spread over all the world. Indeed, they clearly and beyond all doubt taught with us that the Holy Spirit proceeds from the Father. And when a Council was assembled . . . the legates sent as vicars of Holy Pope John, as though he were himself present and giving forth the true doctrine of the Trinity with us, confirmed the Creed of Faith which is professed and believed by the concord of all the Ecumenical Councils in agreement with the words of the Lord, and they approved it with the same meaning and doctrine, both by word and speech and with the signature of their own hand.[38]

Reading between the lines of this statement, it appears that some discussion of the problem of the procession of the Holy Spirit took place before the Council convened. This would corroborate the evidence from Pope John's letter. It would also appear that the papal legates signed such a statement not because it did not deny the procession from the Son but because they understood through previous discussions the Byzantine position on the theological implications of the *Filioque* doctine as well as the *Filioque* addition to the Creed.

Thus, as far as Photius was concerned, "the Roman Church [was] in unity with the four other Patriarchal Sees."[39] How then, asks Photius, is it possible for those imitators of Ham to defy the authority of Christ, the authority of the

---

[37]*PG* 102, 816 and 818.
[38]*PG* 102, 820.
[39]*PG* 102, 820.

Ecumenical Councils and the authority of the Roman See?

Photius uses rather sharp language when referring to the Carolingian theologians whom he considers the "imitators of Ham." He claims a "veil of ignorance is cast over them,"[40] that they are men of "depraved mind,"[41] that they are in an "abyss of error,"[42] and that the "insanity of their heresy"[43] has introduced "perversion" into theology[44] which "slanders the dignity of the Holy Spirit."[45]

---

[40] *PG* 102, 797.
[41] *PG* 102, 805.
[42] *PG* 102, 804.
[43] *PG* 102, 808.
[44] *PG* 102, 809.
[45] *PG* 102, 797.

CHAPTER XI

Photius' *Mystagogia*

In 886 Photius was deposed by his former pupil, now Emperor Leo VI (886-912), and replaced by the Emperor's brother Stephen (886-893). Photius, in exile, completed his work on the procession of the Holy Spirit, the *Mystagogia*.[1] In exile, however, Photius did not have access to his library and his secretaries. He may not have had access any longer to the assumed Greek translations of the Carolingian works and hence may have been treating the subject from memory.

Photius did not consider his *Mystagogia* a full treatment of the subject. At the end of the work he acknowledges that it is just a summary of "basic points of information."[2] "If ever the Lord restores to me," writes Photius, "the books and secretaries taken from me, perhaps, with the aid of the Spirit . . . you will . . . have a refutation of their claims . . .

---

[1] In studying the original text of the *Mystagogia,* I have used a handwritten French translation by Fr. John Meyendorff. I wish to express my gratitude to him for having placed his work at my disposal.

[2] *PG* 102, 389.

and also the most . . . irrefragable testimony of our wisest blessed Fathers by which the opinion of this apostasy is refuted and convicted of blasphemy."[3]

The Theological Critique of the *Filioque*

In his *Mystagogia* Photius immediately appeals to the highest authority, to that "voice which says the Holy Spirit proceeds from the Father."[4] That voice is none other than the Son himself "who established in his own sacred teaching ... the fact that the Spirit proceeds from the Father."[5]

Photius informs the proponents of the *Filioque* that it is "not too late . . . to become aware of [their] impieties [and] to conform in thought to the teaching of the Catholic and Apostolic Church. . . ."[6]

> It is not too late for your entire spirit and your reason . . . to learn to believe the following realities: the Persons of the divine and consubstantial Trinity are united by an inexpressible and indefectible communion of nature, but in the *mode of the hypostases* each preserves unchangeable his own personal properties in relation to the others . . . As their communion of nature does not admit a single division or a single distinction, so also that which constitutes the personal character of each hypostasis never enters in any way into any confusion... Just as the Son is born of the Father and lives unchangeable in himself, preserving his dignity of Son, so also the Most Holy Spirit proceeds from the Father and lives unchangeable in himself, preserving his faculty of proceeding from the Father. Thus, the Spirit, coming forth from the un-caused Father . . . [retains] the eternal character of his procession. So also the Son, who is born of the un-caused Father, would not know how to be the origin of any birth or any procession... He would not know how to distort his privilege of being Son by introducing some new relation.[7]

---

[3]*PG* 102, 389.
[4]*PG* 102, 280 and 281.
[5]*PG* 102, 280 and 281.
[6]*PG* 102, 324.
[7]*PG* 102, 324 and 326.

For Photius this is the central fact of revealed triadology. Photius develops several arguments against the doctrine of the *Filioque,* some of which he touched on in his Encyclical and in his letter to the Patriarch of Aquileia. Although he often repeats himself and does not move logically from one thought to the next, it is not difficult to systematize his essential arguments.

One of his most repeated arguments is that if both the Son and the Spirit come forth from the same cause, which is the un-caused Father, and if, "as that blasphemy proclaims,"[8] the Son is also a cause of the Spirit, then one is logically forced "to assert that the Spirit must also produce the Son."[9] His idea is that there should be a reciprocity of cause between the Son and the Spirit. If the Son is a cause of the Spirit, why is the Spirit not also a cause of the Son?

Connected with the above argument is the idea that the Spirit, if he proceeds from the Father and the Son, would be both generated and proceeding.

> If the Spirit proceeds from the Son, but not earlier or later than the Son is generated from the Father . . . at that same moment the Spirit certainly proceeds from the Son. If then, while the Son comes forth by generation, the Son produces the Holy Spirit by procession. It would then follow that he . . . came into being with the Son . . . While then the Son is being generated, it would follow that at the same moment the Spirit was also being generated together with the Son and was proceeding from him. The Spirit would therefore be simultaneously generated and proceeding. Generated because he would be coming forth together with the generated Son but proceeding because he would undergo a double procession.[10]

Photius admits that the proponents of the *Filioque* recognize that the Son's begetting does not impair the "ineffable simplicity of the Father."[11] But, he asks, if the

---

[8] *PG* 102, 281.
[9] *PG* 102, 281 and 284.
[10] *PG* 102, 341 and 344.
[11] *PG* 102, 284.

Spirit has a double cause, "will not composition be the result?... How will simplicity in the Trinity retain its dignity?"[12] If the Spirit proceeds from the Son, then, according to Photius, the particular property of the uncaused Father "would be stripped and emptied of reason; the property which uniquely characterizes him would no longer be exclusively his own and two Divine Persons . . . would be confused in one Person."[13] Not only would two Persons be merged into one, but even the Person of the Father would be divided in itself.

> One cannot escape the fact that this impious doctrine divides even the hypostasis of the Father in two. Or it establishes the fact that the Person of the Son does not have origin except in part from that which is of the Father.... If the Son is the cause of the Spirit, ... then it would be necessary to admit that either the Son is a part of the hypostasis of the Father because he possesses the faculty of being the cause or that the Son completes the Person of the Father who, consequently, would not yet be fully realized and hence would be imperfect. The Son then would be nothing but a part of the Father and the awesome mystery of the Trinity would be cut into a dyad.[14]

If one admits two causes in the Trinity, then the divine monarchy of the Trinity is destroyed. Photius contends that this leads to polytheism and then to atheism.[15] "If two causes combine themselves in the monarchical Trinity, why, then, according to the same reasoning, does not a third one appear? In fact, once the principle, which is above all principles, is upset . . . this principle is divided into a dyad and it could be applied to the entire Trinity."[16] But, argues Photius, it is precisely the Triadological principle which has been revealed and not a Dyadic principle.[17]

---

[12]*PG* 102, 284.
[13]*PG* 102, 289.
[14]*PG* 102, 293 and 295.
[15]*PG* 102, 292.
[16]*PG* 102, 292.
[17]*PG* 102, 292.

The Father is the un-caused Cause of the Trinity not by nature or essence but by his hypostatical character.[18] Procession is personal and not essential;[19] it belongs to the personal property of only the Father and cannot be common.

> If whatever is in God is not seen in the unity and consubstantiality of the omnipotent Trinity, it clearly belongs to only one of the Three Persons. And the procession of the Spirit is not [common]... It is, therefore, of only one of the Three Persons.[20]

The proponents of the *Filioque* consider the procession of the Holy Spirit as a common activity of the Father and the Son. "If so, then the Spirit himself would participate in his own procession. He would be partially producer and partially produced, partially the cause and partially caused."[21] Not only would the Person of the Father and Son be merged into one Person and the Person of the Father cut in two, but the oneness of the Spirit would also be cut in two.[22]

Not only would the Spirit proceed from himself, if the common nature is the principle of procession, but the Spirit would also have to participate in the generation of the Son and, most importantly, why could not another person proceed from the Spirit?[23] "How would one find a way which would exclude the Spirit from producing another person because it would be in conformity with his position of equal consubstantiality with the Father and the Son."[24]

An idea which Photius first touched upon in his Encyclical and later in his letter to the Patriarch of Aquileia is further developed in the *Mystagogia*. If the Spirit proceeds from the Son, "what then does he gain that he does not already

---

[18] *PG* 102, 293.
[19] *PG* 102, 316 and 317.
[20] *PG* 102, 341.
[21] *PG* 102, 288.
[22] *PG* 102, 341.
[23] *PG* 102, 317.
[24] *PG* 102, 289.

possess in his procession from the Father?"[25] If the Spirit receives something "additional" from his procession from the Son, must one not admit that the Spirit was imperfect before receiving this "addition"? Must one not also admit that the Father himself is not perfect?

> If the procession of the Spirit from the Father is perfect, and it is, because it is a perfect God who proceeds from a perfect God, what then does the procession from the Son add? If it adds something, it is necessary to state what it adds.[26] ... This theory is absolutely of no usefulness neither for the Son, nor for anyone ... there is no way he can gain from it.[27]

If the procession of the Spirit is not the property of the Father, then it will assuredly not be the Son's.[28] The proponents of the *Filioque* claim that the principle of procession is not personal but essential; that is, the principle of procession belongs to the Divine essence. Thus, argues Photius, procession is logically a common element in the Trinity and the Triadic principle of Persons is destroyed. According to their system, the property of the person of the Father is dissolved in nature, suppressing totally the unique un-caused Cause in the Trinity of Persons.[29] There is, according to their system, a logical interchange of the properties of Persons, and hence it logically follows that the Father must in some way be the object of generation, since the Father and the Son share their personal properties.[30]

Photius also maintains that the proponents of the *Filioque* exclude the Spirit from the life of love which is common to the Father and the Son.

---

[25] *PG* 102, 288.
[26] *PG* 102, 312 and 314.
[27] *PG* 102, 320 and 321.
[28] *PG* 102, 296.
[29] *PG* 102, 297.
[30] *PG* 102, 297.

> These people . . . have introduced another innovation: that which the Father and Son have in common they have excluded from the Spirit. But it is by nature [in their system] and not by . . . their hypostatical properties that the Father and Son are in common. They have thus rejected the consubstantial Spirit from the common nature of the Father.[31]

If the Spirit proceeds from the Father and the Son, then the Spirit is distinguished by more properties than the Son. The Son then "is closer to the nature of the Father. The Spirit, equal in honor to the Father, is then injured because two properties distinguish him from the Father."[32]

Photius maintains that the *Filioque* doctrine leads to semi-Sabellianism,[33] polytheism,[34] to the heresy of Macedonius,[35] and to pagan mythology.[36] He also claims that the *Filioque* doctrine leads both to Tetralogy and Dyadology[37] rather than Triadology, ultimately bringing Christian Revelation to ridicule and jest.[38]

The Response to Carolingian Exegesis

In handling the Biblical material used by the Carolingians in support of the *Filioque* doctrine, Photius concentrates on their main ideas and their most frequently used texts, especially those used by Ratramnus. His first concern is with the text from the Gospel of John[39] which states that the Spirit "will take of mine and announce it to you."

---

[31]*PG* 102, 313.
[32]*PG* 102, 313.
[33]*PG* 102, 289.
[34]*PG* 102, 292.
[35]*PG* 102, 313.
[36]*PG* 102, 321.
[37]*PG* 102, 321.
[38]*PG* 102, 340.
[39]John 16:14.

> Who will not see that you have recourse to this statement of the Saviour not to find an advocate [of your teaching] but to dare to accuse the Saviour himself of error, the ineffable source of Truth? . . . In fact, the Creator and Sustainer of the human race teaches that the Spirit proceeds from the Father *without in any way adding to it that he proceeds from himself also*. He affirms that the Father is the unique Cause both of his own generation and of the procession of the Holy Spirit. But, according to you, when he announces that "he will take from that which is mine," he therefore suppresses through his profound silence his first doctrine. Thus, you claim that in mentioning the first, he then reconciles the two opposing theories. But, in fact, while, according to you, he has done this, he, in fact, did not.[40]

Photius strikes at the heart of the Latin interpretation which was developed by Augustine in his *Tractatus in Joannis Evangelium* and in his *Contra Maximinum* and then repeated by Ratramnus. Augustine's position was that Christ did not deny that the Spirit proceeds from him because he remained silent. Photius claims that their effort to turn this text into a support for the doctrine of the procession of the Spirit from the Son is futile. "Is taking something from someone the same as to proceed...?"[41]

> The Lord did not say "he will take from me" but "he will take from that which is mine." . . . There is a great and profound difference between the two expressions "of mine" and "of me." . . . In fact, the expression "of me" introduces in the action the same subject who pronounces the phrase; the expression "of mine" introduces another person, different from the subject of the phrase. And who is this [person], if not the Father from whom the Spirit "takes" something? . . . In fact, school children know that the expression "of me" implies the same subject who pronounces the phrase, while the expression "of mine" announces another Person united by intimate bonds to the subject but personally different from him.[42]

> According to your own personal opinion, you have charged [the Lord] with precisely three calumnies: you have made him say what he did not say, denied what he said, and have taught an idea which not only does not follow from his words but which, to the contrary, he combats...[43]

---

[40]*PG* 102, 300.
[41]*PG* 102, 300.
[42]*PG* 102, 301.
[43]*PG* 102, 304.

Photius argues that the reason the Son made this statement had nothing to do with the procession of the Spirit. "Listen well, o man, to the words of the Saviour: why will he take? Why? In order to "announce to you the things to come.' "[44]

In analyzing the statement that "all that the Father has is mine," Photius unites it with the previous idea. "Thus, he who takes that which is mine, takes also that which is my Father's . . . he continues to clarify it. . . . 'This is why I said he takes of mine because in the Father there is that which is mine; the Spirit takes from the Father and that which is the Father's is mine.' "[45] The Son, writes Photius, seems to say that "when I say 'of mine' you should raise your spirits towards the Father."[46] "Is there anything more clearly demonstrable? The expression 'He will take of mine' sends us back to the Person of the Father. . . .' "[47]

Photius is quite aware that the Carolingians, mainly Ratramnus, stressed the idea that the Son received the power to produce the Spirit from the Father. But, asks Photius, why did the Son receive this privilege? "Whence comes this unjust favor which gives the Son the [privilege] of being a cause of the procession of the Spirit, while the Spirit, who originates with an equal rank and with equal honor of the same nature, is stripped of equal privileges?"[48]

> You will object perhaps . . . But why did not the Son himself, in producing the Spirit who is consubstantial with him, accord him [the Spirit] the faculty and the honor which he has received, so that the Spirit could also have the glory of producing a consubstantial Person?[49]

Photius deals at length with those Biblical texts used by the Carolingians which state that the Spirit proceeds from

---

[44] *PG* 102, 309 and 312.
[45] *PG* 102, 309 and 312.
[46] *PG* 102, 309 and 312.
[47] *PG* 102, 312.
[48] *PG* 102, 317.
[49] *PG* 102, 320.

the Son because the Spirit is the Spirit "of the Son." Because Paul wrote that the Spirit is "of the Son" and because he wrote that "God has sent into your hearts the Spirit of his Son,"[50] the proponents of the *Filioque* claim that Paul taught the doctrine of the procession of the Spirit from the Son. "In what place, then, did Paul say that the Spirit 'proceeds from the Son?' He said that the Spirit is 'of the Son' and nothing else."[51]

> He said 'the Spirit of the Son,' [and] this is correct and divine. But why do you falsify these words and not say what he said?... 'The Spirit of the Son'—he could have said nothing better. The Spirit . . . is of the same essence as the Son; he is consubstantial with him.... In saying 'the Spirit of the Son' Paul affirms their complete identity of nature, but has no intention of introducing an idea about the cause of the procession of the Spirit . . . he gives not a glimpse of any idea of cause.[52]

Photius finds the Latin interpretation of "of the Son" both grammatically and conceptually primitive. To be consistent, argues Photius, they would have to assert that the Father is begotten by the Son because the Father is the Father "of the Son." According to the Byzantine position, the Father is the "Father of the Son" not because [the Father] is born from [the Son], but because he is consubstantial with him.[53]

> When we affirm that the Spirit is of the Father and the Son, we declare that he is entirely consubstantial with each of them. We know he is consubstantial with the Father because he proceeds from him; [we know] he is consubstantial with the Son *not* because he proceeds from the Son . . . but because each of them comes forth equally from a unique, indivisible and eternal Cause.[54]
>
> 'The Spirit of the Son.' Understand, o man, and distort no longer the divine and salvific words of the harbinger of Truth.... 'The

---

[50]*PG* 102, 328.
[51]*PG* 102, 328 and 329.
[52]*PG* 102, 329.
[53]*PG* 102, 329.
[54]*PG* 102, 332.

Spirit of his Son' has one meaning [and] 'the Spirit who proceeds from the Son' has another meaning.[55]

Photius demonstrates what he considers the conceptual and grammatical primitiveness of the Latin interpretation by giving numerous examples from Scripture which state that the Spirit is the Spirit "of" something. The Holy Spirit is called the Spirit of wisdom, of intelligence, of knowledge, of love, of temperance, of humility, of faith, of hope, of strength, of revelation, of counsel, of piety, of gentleness, of meekness, of perception, of judgment, of fire and of plenitude. Does the Spirit therefore proceed from these?[56]

Photius and the Latin Fathers

Photius admits that Augustine and other Latin Fathers, obviously from the texts submitted to Photius, taught the *Filioque*. But Photius is ready to go to great extremes to protect the Latin Fathers. He asks "how can one be certain that after the lapse of all these years their writings have not been distorted...?"[57] Even if their authentic works contain this teaching, they are not guilty because the charge was never brought before them by the Church. But now that the question has been brought before the Church the Carolingian theologians, in using the Latin Fathers as authorities, accuse themselves and injure their Fathers.[58] Since the Ecumenical Councils declared that the Spirit proceeds from the Father, and since this was recently confirmed,[59] are the

---

[55]*PG* 102, 332.
[56]*PG* 102, 333.
[57]*PG* 102, 352.
[58]*PG* 102, 344 and 345.
[59]The reference is to the Council of 879-880.

Latin Fathers delighted to be in error on this issue?[60] Photius urges them to leave the Latin Fathers in peace.

> If, [and] such is the human condition, though otherwise adorned with very fine virtues, they . . . slipped, either because of a certain ignorance or by negligence, . . . what is this to you?[61]

Photius refers specifically to the fact that, although some of the Latin Fathers taught the *Filioque,* they had no intention of adding it to the Ecumenical Creed.

> Since they have not become even slight participators in those things with which you abound, but rather are adorned with many examples of admirable virtue and piety and professed your teaching either through ignorance or negligence, why do you set up for yourself this human defect as a law of blasphemous believing and by that law of yours declare them unjust violators—men who have sanctioned nothing of this sort—and judge them guilty of extreme blasphemy under the mask of benevolence and love? The fruits of *your studies and attempts* are not good.[62]

Photius claims that the Carolingian appeal to the Latin Fathers is parricidal, for they oppose the teaching of the Latin Fathers to the teaching of the Lord and the decrees of the Ecumenical Councils.[63] Instead of acting like parricides, Photius recommends another course of action.

> [The Fathers] were human and no one made of dust and ephemeral nature can preserve himself forever immune from every human error. . . . Though . . . they by chance fell into something shameful and unbecoming, I for my part would imitate the good sons of Noah and hide my father's shame, using silence and gratitude in place of a covering. I would not follow Ham's example as you do. Indeed, much more . . . impudently than he, you publish the shame of those you call your Fathers. [Ham] was cursed not because he uncovered his father but because he did not cover him. You, however, both uncover your Fathers and glory in your boldness. [Ham] tells the secret to his brothers. You proclaim yours not to brothers . . . but make the whole world your theater.[64]

---

[60]*PG* 102, 345.
[61]*PG* 102, 345 and 348.
[62]*PG* 102, 348.
[63]*PG* 102, 348 and 349.
[64]*PG* 102, 349 and 352.

Photius finds another way of protecting the Latin Fathers. "How is it that you take as *dogma* and law what they did not [teach] in the sense of *dogma?*"[65] Indeed, Photius' defense of Augustine coincides precisely with Augustine's own request in his concluding prayer of *De Trinitate*. "O Lord the one God," wrote Augustine, "God the Trinity, whatever I have said in these books that is of Thine, may they acknowledge who are Thine; if anything of my own, may it be pardoned both by Thee and by those who are Thine."[66] Augustine clearly never intended to impose his system of triadology on the Church.

Photius, full of genuine sympathy for the Latin Fathers, maintains that it is quite easy to fall into error on some issues, especially if one is directing his energies toward combatting other heresies. Photius gives several examples of illustrious Fathers who missed "the exact norm of truth" on certain issues.[67] Included in this list are Dionysius of Alexandria, Methodius, Irenaeus, Hippolytus and even Basil the Great.

Photius and the Roman Popes

Although he protects the Latin Fathers as fully as possible, Photius counters their teaching by appealing to the authority of the Roman Bishops.

> Ambrose said the Spirit proceeds from the Son . . . but Damasus . . . opposes [this]. In confirming the Second Council . . . , he professes clearly that the Spirit proceeds from the Father. Ambrose and Augustine said.... But Celestine did not say this...[68]

---

[65]*PG* 102, 352 and 353.
[66]*De Trinitate* XV, 28, 51.
[67]*PG* 102, 356 and 357.
[68]*PG* 102, 360.

Leo the Great . . . the pillar of the Fourth Council both through his dogmatic letters . . . and through his legates . . . gives the same example of Orthodoxy not only in the entire West but also in the lands of the East. He teaches in very clear words that the Spirit proceeds from the Father. Not only that, but he also pronounces that those who dare to teach anything except the Council's decision be deprived of their priestly office.[69]

Think of the distinguished Vigilius. . . . He too attended the Fifth Council[70] . . . and pronounced . . . that the Most Holy and consubstantial Spirit proceeds from the Father.[71]

The good and just Agatho . . . made the Sixth Council prominent and illustrious. . . . And he kept the Creed of our pure, sincere faith. . . . He consigned to equal condemnation those who dared to remove any of the items which had been sanctioned.[72]

How shall I pass over in silence the Roman Popes Gregory and Zachary. . . . For though neither sat at Ecumenical Councils, yet they taught openly and clearly . . . that the Most Holy Spirit proceeds from the Father.[73]

The Roman Popes and the Creed

Photius appeals to Pope Leo III as an example of Rome's position on the subject of adding to the Creed. But Photius' account is not thoroughly accurate and betrays Photius' attitude toward the Latin language.

Recently (the second generation has not yet passed) that very celebrated Leo . . . removed all pretext of heresy from all. Because of the poverty of the Latin language, which is not as rich as the Greek, the Latins, in conveying the sacred doctrine of our Fathers, did not use words purely, sincerely or aptly . . . their great poverty of

---

[69]*PG* 102, 361.

[70]This is historically inaccurate, for Pope Vigilius did not *attend* the Fifth Ecumenical Council.

[71]*PG* 102, 365 and 368.

[72]*PG* 102, 368.

[73]*PG* 102, 368.

vocabulary for expressing an idea precisely . . . created . . . a suspicion of diversity of faith—for that reason the . . . very holy man conceived the idea (the reason he conceived the idea was because of that heresy we have already mentioned, which is now preached openly but was then whispered in Rome) [and] commanded that the Romans also recite the Creed of Faith in Greek. By this divinely inspired plan he . . . repaired the poverty of Latin and removed from Catholics the suspicion of a difference in faith and also uprooted entirely from Rome the impiety recently thriving there. He therefore placed notices and edicts that not only in Rome but also in all the provinces which belonged to the Roman Pontificate . . . the sacred Creed of our Faith should be recited in Greek, as it had been enunciated from the beginning by synodical statements and decrees, even by those who spoke Latin. In speeches and synodical letters he ordered this and strengthened the firmness of dogma by the dread chains of anathema.[74]

Photius maintains that his successors—Popes Leo IV (847-855) and Benedict III (855-858)—[Photius may be confusing the two Leos] retained the policy of Leo III. Under Pope Leo [ostensibly the IV] again the problem of the procession of the Spirit was raised. He therefore "brought forth the . . . shields . . . in Greek . . . [and] ordered them to be read in the presence of the Roman people and to be exposed for all to see."[75] Photius claims that "many of those who saw and read them are even now among the living."[76]

Once again Photius refers to the signatures of the papal legates at the Council of 879-880.

My John also—(for he is mine both for other reasons and because he supported me more than others)—my John, then . . . through his pious and illustrious legates Paul, Eugenius, and Peter . . . who attended our Council, like his predecessors in the Catholic Church of God, the Roman Bishops, accepted the Creed of Faith with the mind, tongue, and sacred hands of those very illustrious and admirable men whom we have mentioned and subscribed to it and signed it. Indeed, also, his successor Hadrian [Hadrian III; 884-885] . . . in his synodical letter . . . taught that the Spirit proceeds from the Father.[77]

---

[74]*PG* 102, 376 and 377.
[75]*PG* 102, 380.
[76]*PG* 102, 380.
[77]*PG* 102, 381.

The Creed as Perfect

In considering the decisions of the Fourth Ecumenical Council, accepted by the Roman Bishops, Photius calls attention to the statement of that Council concerning the "fullness and perfection" of the Creed.

> But it is better to hear the sacred words themselves. The Council states: "This wise and salutary Creed of divine grace will suffice then for full knowledge and confirmation of piety." It says perfect or full.... There is no need to add anything to it or take it away. And how is it perfect? Turn your attention to what follows. It states: "It teaches the perfect doctrine of the Father and the Son and the Holy Spirit." And how does it teach the perfect doctrine? It says the Son is generated from the Father but that the Spirit proceeds from the Father.... Toward the end [it] says: "The Holy and Ecumenical Council has defined." . . . What did it define? "No one is permitted to bring forth another belief or put together or compose or think or teach others. Those who dare to compose another faith or teach or hand down another Creed . . . if they are bishops or clerics, let them be deposed. If monks or laymen, let them be anathematized."[78]

Photius' Conclusion

Photius concludes his *Mystagogia* with four more chapters of analysis of the Latin interpretation of the Spirit's being "of the Son." Photius realized how crucial this was to the Carolingians, especially to Ratramnus. Photius again stresses that the Spirit is "of the Son" because he is consubstantial with the Son. But in his concluding analysis Photius treats the idea of the Spirit's anointing of Christ. The Spirit is the Spirit of the Son because "the Spirit is consubstantial with him and because [the Spirit] anoints him and remains on him and in him."[79]

---

[78]*PG* 102, 363.
[79]*PG* 102, 385.

Photius issues a final warning to the proponents of the *Filioque*, urging them to turn from their dangerous path.

> You refuse to obey Christ and his disciples, refuse to follow the Ecumenical Councils and to exercise your mind with the arguments drawn from sacred reading. Instead you attack the common Lord, you lie against great Paul, you revolt against the Holy Ecumenical Councils, and you calumniate your Fathers and the Roman Bishops. . . . "O dullest of peoples! Fools, when will you be wise?" [Ps. 94:8].[80]

With the last lines of the *Mystagogia* the Byzantine-Carolingian Triadological controversy comes to an end, the conclusions of which must now be discussed.

---

[80]*PG* 102, 389.

CHAPTER XII

Conclusions

On the basis of the research presented in this study, certain historical and theological conclusions follow. The historical conclusions also contain certain aspects of this research which deserve to be summarized and highlighted.

Historical Conclusions

1) It is clear that the architect of *Filioque* theology and *Filioque* Biblical exegesis was Augustine. But, as Augustine stated in his concluding prayer in *De Trinitate,* he never intended to impose his triadological thought on the Church. He considered his triadology as *theologoumenon* and not as dogma. And, of course, he was in no way involved in the addition of the *Filioque* to the Ecumenical Creed. Nevertheless, in a certain sense Photius' response to the Carolingian theologians is also a response to Augustinian triadology.

2) The rapid acceptance of Augustinian triadology in

the Latin West and the simultaneous lack of interest in things Latin by the Byzantine East aided enormously to the later triadological separation of East and West. If the Byzantine East had been more conscious of the "ecumenicity" of the Church, if the Byzantine East had not possessed an arrogant sense of "superiority," it is reasonable to conclude that the works of Augustine might have been translated into Greek. If Augustine's *De Trinitate* had been available to the Greek East, it is quite possible that an Ecumenical Council might have reached an equitable solution of Augustine's interpretation of the *Filioque*.

3) The *Filioque* first entered the Ecumenical Creed in the Latin West by a simple method of transposition and not by any willful act of interpolation in conscious violation of the Ecumenical decrees.

The historical process of the transposition of the *Filioque* to the Ecumenical Creed occurred quite easily. The immense popularity of the Athanasian Creed with its *et Filio* and the existence of the *Filioque* in most of the writings on the Holy Trinity in the post-Augustinian Latin West formed the matrix out of which the transposition occurred. Obviously thinking that the *Filioque* was a part of the original Ecumenical Creed, and perhaps surprised at its omission in certain manuscripts, some Spanish theologians simply transferred the *et Filio* in the form of *Filioque* from the Athanasian Creed to the Ecumenical Creed.

It is quite clear from the Acts of the Council of Toledo that the Ecumenical Creed had already been previously interpolated. The Council of Toledo firmly believed that it was confirming the original Nicene-Constantinopolitan Creed. There is no reason to assume that the existence of the *Filioque* in the Ecumenical Creed at the Council of Toledo was itself a later interpolation of the Acts of this Council, for all the historical influences which could have caused such an interpolation were equally present before and during the time of the Council of Toledo.

That the *Filioque* was consciously and deliberately added

Conclusions

to the Ecumenical Creed in Spain in order to stress, in opposition to Germanic Arianism, the consubstantiality of the Son with the Father seems neither convincing nor historically necessary. After Augustine there was a natural development of the *Filioque* in Latin theology. That many considered *Filioque* theology efficacious in the struggle with Germanic Arianism seems undeniable. But the transposition of the *Filioque* to the Ecumenical Creed does not necessarily presuppose the historical background of Arianism.

4) It is significant that each time the Greek East confronted the *Filioque*, there was an energetic reaction. This occurred with the alleged *Filioque* expression of Pope Martin, with the Latin monks on Mount Olivet, and with Photius' reaction to the use of the interpolated Creed in Bulgaria. When the Latin monks wrote to Pope Leo III that the Greeks "view that phrase [i.e. the *Filioque*] which we say as a *serious* matter," they were not overstating the problem.

5) Because the *Filioque* question was so bound up with the concomitant political and cultural estrangement between the Greek East and the Latin West, the importance of the Iconoclastic heresy cannot be overlooked. Iconoclasm, together with the rapid advance of the Lombards, forced the Roman Popes to seek out the Franks as the new "protectors" of Rome. One could argue that if the Greek East had not fallen into Iconoclasm, the axis of political order might not have shifted from Rome-Constantinople to Rome-Aachen. According to such an argument, the Greek East would have to share indirectly in the responsibility of the later Frankish influence over Rome. Thus, indirectly the heresy of Iconoclasm helped sow the seeds for what the Byzantine East would later regard as the heresy of the *Filioque*.

Also of historical significance for the shift of the political order to an alliance between Rome and the Franks is the method ultimately resorted to by Pope Stephen to force King Pippin to destroy the Lombard menace. After other methods and appeals had failed, Pope Stephen resorted to writing to Pippin in the name of St. Peter himself, threatening Pippin with eternal damnation if he did not come to the aid of Rome. The result of the letter was Pippin's decisive action against the Lombards and his donation of the Exarchate of Ravenna to the Pope. This complicated the progressive political, cultural, and theological estrangement between Rome and Constantinople.

6) It is noteworthy that the *Libri Carolini* use the same accusation against Patriarch Tarasius' profession of faith as the Byzantine East later uses against the *Filioque*. According to the *Libri Carolini,* the *per Filium* was illegitimate because it was an unauthorized interpolation of the Nicene-Constantinopolitan Creed. It is also noteworthy that the author of the *Libri Carolini* uses another argument against the *per Filium* which contradicts his own doctrine of the *Filioque* and which Photius, without dependency of course, later uses as one of his main arguments against the *Filioque*. The author of the *Libri Carolini* claims that "in order to proceed from the Father, the Holy Spirit does not need the help of another."

Two arguments in the *Libri Carolini* are "creatively" unique. That the Spirit cannot proceed from the Father through the Son because, in accordance with John 1:3, this would imply that the Spirit is a creature is a rather unusual argument. The argument based on an analogy between the physical birth of Christ and the eternal procession of the Spirit is also quite unique: since the Son was born from [*ex*] humanity and not through [*per*] humanity, it is therefore theologically unsound to say that the Spirit proceeds through the Son.

Of peripheral historical significance is the indirect evidence in this section of the *Libri Carolini* which tends to indicate the Spanish origin of the author. The author's references to Isidore of Seville and Vigilius of Thapsus, also referred to in Theodulf's *De Spiritu Sancto,* and the author's certainty that the *Filioque* was a part of the original

Conclusions

Creed seem to add to the already overwhelming evidence recently brought forth by Ann Freeman that the dominant author of the *Libri Carolini* was Theodulf of Orléans.

7) Although the Council of Frankfurt, considered "ecumenical" or "universal" by many Franks, may have sanctioned the *Filioque* addition to the Creed, the first really creative work of a *theology of interpolation* was done by Paulinus of Aquileia at the Council of Friuli. During the entire scope of the Byzantine-Carolingian Triadological controversy three attempts at a *theology of interpolation* emerge.

Paulinus' *theology of interpolation* is of enormous significance not only because it was the first Carolingian attempt but also because it was worked out in full awareness of the opposition of the Roman See. Paulinus knew that the *Filioque* was neither in the Nicene nor the Nicene-Constantinopolitan Creed; and he knew that Rome had not added the *Filioque* to the Creed and that Rome was quite opposed to any alteration of the Creed.

Although Paulinus is aware that one of the Ecumenical Councils prohibited any alteration of the "Nicene" Creed, he is not certain whether it was the Council of Nicaea itself. Historically there is no evidence that the Council of Nicaea prohibited any addition, subtraction, or alteration of the "Nicene" Creed. Canon VII of the Third Ecumenical Council explicitly prohibited a different *faith* other than that established by the Council of Nicaea. The Fourth Ecumenical Council explicitly prohibited not only a different *faith* but also a different *Creed* other than the Nicene-Constantinopolitan. Thus, when Paulinus argues that the Second Ecumenical Council established the precedent for future additions to the Creed by adding when such alterations had been prohibited, he is arguing retroactively. Nevertheless, the very fact that the Second Ecumenical Council did add to the Creed means, according to Paulinus, that the precedent had been established and that, in fact, the Creed could be added to.

According to Paulinus' *theology of interpolation,* any

addition to the Creed must meet two criteria: 1) the addition must not contradict the *intention* of the Fathers; and 2) the addition must have as its objective the destruction of a heresy. It is noteworthy that Paulinus does not distinguish between the authority of an "Ecumenical" council and the authority of a "local" council, unless, of course, he considered the Council of Frankfurt as Ecumenical. Even more remarkable is the fact that the authority of the Roman See plays no role in Paulinus' *theology of interpolation,* unless, of course, the objective of his *theology of interpolation* was to win the support of Rome.

The second Carolingian *theology of interpolation* was improvised by the Frankish envoys in discussion with Pope Leo III. According to the Frankish envoys, one ought to be able to add to the Creed provided that 1) those adding have good will; and 2) the objective of the addition is an attempt to make what is "good" even "better." The Frankish envoys add to their *theology of interpolation* their assumption that the end of the world is near and hence it is important for all Christians to know, for the sake of their salvation, that the Spirit proceeds also from the Son.

The third and most sophisticated Carolingian *theology of interpolation* was developed by Ratramnus of Corbie. In connection with Ratramnus' *theology of interpolation* it must be stressed that Pope Nicholas inadvertently misled the Carolingian theologians on one issue. In his letter to Hincmar Pope Nicholas wrote that the Greeks accuse us "because we say that the Holy Spirit proceeds from the Father and the Son while they maintain that he proceeds from the Father only." Further in his letter he writes: "As to the procession of the Holy Spirit—who does not know that illustrious men, particularly Latins, have written treatises by whose authority we can make a sane response to their insanity...." Pope Nicholas, although consciously giving papal endorsement to the *doctrine* of the *Filioque,* never refers to the Creed and the addition of the *Filioque* to it. Rome had not interpolated the Creed, but Ratramnus simply assumed from the papal endorsement of the *Filioque doctrine*

Conclusions

that Rome had interpolated the Creed by papal authority. Ratramnus' *theology of interpolation* hinges on this false assumption.

According to Ratramnus, if the Second Ecumenical Council added to the original Creed, establishing the precedent for future additions, then certainly the Bishop of Rome has *at least* that right. Ratramnus' *theology of interpolation* is therefore ultimately rooted in his view of the primacy of the Bishop of Rome. Although Ratramnus argues from a false historical assumption, there is an intrinsic logic to his *theology of interpolation*, if one accepts his interpretation of papal primacy. The *Filioque* addition to the Creed is "legitimate," according to Ratramnus, because it was added by the authority of the Roman See.

8) Although it cannot be considered a *theology of interpolation*, there is a remarkable "newstep," a unique argument in the *Libellus de Processione Spiritus Sancti* which attempts to prove that the *Filioque* doctrine had the sanction and authority of both the Ecumenical Councils and the See of Rome. The writer of the *Libellus* maintains that since the Fifth Ecumenical Council approved "*in every way*" the writings of Augustine, then the triadological thought of Augustine, including the *Filioque*, received "Ecumenical" sanction. Since the Fifth Ecumenical Council was accepted by Rome, the *Filioque* was therefore also sanctioned by Rome.

9) Some noteworthy conclusions can be drawn from Pope Leo's meeting with the Frankish envoys. Pope Leo, although believing in the *doctrine* of the *Filioque*, absolutely refused the *Filioque's* interpolation in the Ecumenical Creed. He regarded the interpolated *Filioque* as "illicit" and, most interestingly, did not believe that he had the authority to alter the decisions of the Fathers. "I shall not say that I prefer myself to the Fathers. And far be it from me to count myself their equal," he states. Unlike Ratramnus, Pope Leo seems to think that he does not have "at least" the same right or authority as the Ecumenical Councils. Any

alteration of the Creed, argues Pope Leo, must be done by "competent persons" at "opportune times or places." This respect which Pope Leo had for the traditional authority of Ecumenical Councils and his ostensibly restricted view of papal authority seem to cast doubt on his alleged participation in the forged *Donation of Constantine.*

It is noteworthy that Pope Leo, in requesting that the Franks stop singing the Creed in order not to disturb the people while the *Filioque* is being removed, actually attempts to stop both the addition of the *Filioque* and the custom of singing the Creed. "... In so far as can be done, both things could be dispensed with."

Pope Leo warns the Franks to be cautious "lest by rashly presuming beyond what [one] ought," they "corrupt what was good in itself."

Pope Leo's strong stand against the Frankish envoys tends to cast doubt on the assumption by some that he was essentially of weak character and that he was only a passive tool of Charlemagne and/or of Charlemagne's court in the coronation event.

The recent research by Vittorio Peri confirms the historicity of the two shields which Pope Leo had erected with the original text of the Nicene-Constantinopolitan Creed in both Greek and Latin.

10) Other unique "creative" Carolingian arguments supporting the *Filioque* doctrine emerged as a result of the Byzantine-Carolingian Triadological controversy. In his *De Spiritu Sancto* Theodulf maintained that since the Spirit proceeds from God [*Deus*], the Spirit must also proceed from the Son because the name "Son" cannot be excluded from God. Smaragdus, following a line of thought developed by Pope Gregory's Biblical exegesis, claimed that the Spirit is the mouth of the Son and hence proceeds from him. Ratramnus, arguing from the Biblical text which states that the words of Christ are "Spirit and life," claims that this indicates the Spirit's procession from the Son. Ratramnus also seems to be the first to call attention to the Latin text of

Conclusions 167

John 8:42 which quotes Christ as saying "ego ex Deo *processi et veni.*" What Ratramnus does with this text is most unique. Since Scripture uses the word "procession" in relation to the Son, then the Second Ecumenical Council did not actually distinguish between the way the Son comes forth from the Father and the way the Spirit comes forth from the Father. By adding the term "procession" to the Creed, the Second Ecumenical Council, according to Ratramnus, did not safeguard the distinction between the Son and the Spirit. Hence, the only proper way that the person of the Son can be distinguished from the person of the Spirit is by the *Filioque* doctrine. Ratramnus was unfortunately unaware that the original Greek word [ἐξῆλθον] was not an equivalent of the Greek terminology for procession.

11) Ratramnus' most unusual proposal for a solution of the problem cannot be overlooked. If the Greeks remove what the Second Ecumenical Council added to the original Nicene Creed, then perhaps the Roman Church will remove what they have added.

12) Photius, Pope Nicholas, Aeneas and Ratramnus all consider the new controversy as a "war" which is demonically inspired. Smaragdus, however, believes that the new controversy is "divinely inspired."

13) Pope Nicholas and Aeneas claim that the Roman See never fell into heresy, obviously forgetting Pope Honorius' role in Monothelitism and his condemnation at the Sixth Ecumenical Council.[1]

14) For Aeneas truth somehow resides in the Latin language which expresses the norm of faith; for Photius the Latin language is incapable of fully expressing revealed

---

[1] Mansi 11, 622, 635, 655, 666. His writings were condemned and he himself was posthumously anathematized and excommunicated.

truth and truth therefore is best expressed in the Greek language.

15) During the second phase of the Byzantine-Carolingian Triadological controversy, Alcuin, who had freely admitted that he was not original, becomes an "authority" in his own right.

16) *The* patristic authority for the Carolingian theologians is Augustine. No Church Father is quoted as often or at such great length as is Augustine. Although the Carolingian theologians also appeal to other authorities, the response of the Council of Worms is unique in that it thought the testimony of Augustine alone was sufficient.

17) The question has often been asked: what "sources" did Photius use in his attack on the *Filioque;* where did he receive his knowledge of Latin triadology? There seems to be little doubt that the Carolingians supplied Photius with the sources.

Photius obviously had some knowledge prior to 866 of the differences between the Franks and the Greek East on the question of the procession of the Holy Spirit.

> Now, the procession of the Holy Ghost does not seem to have been an issue between the Eastern and Western Churches until their missionaries fell afoul of one another in Bulgaria in the year 866. That does not, of course, enable us to say that Photius was unaware of the question before 866; for even if he was ignorant of the previous controversies on that score in the West, he could have known of the clash that occurred at Jerusalem in 808 between the Benedictines of the Mount of Olives and the Greek monks of St. Sabas. In 813 there arrived at Constantinople many Palestinian monks, among them St. Michael Syncellus and the brothers Theodore and Theophanes Grapti who were apparently intending to proceed to Rome in order to represent to the Pope the Oriental position on the *Filioque* dispute. They were, however, detained at Constantinople, and never pursued their journey to the West. St. Michael became after 843 abbot of an important monastery at Constantinople, which position he held until his death in 846.

Thus Photius could easily have had contact with several prominent Palestinian monks who had been personally involved in the *Filioque* controversy.[2]

These Palestinian monks were presumably to respond to Pope Leo's letter to the Eastern Churches, for, according to the historical evidence, that was the only dogmatic work on the defense of the *doctrine* of the *Filioque* which was sent to Jerusalem. Thus, Photius may have been well informed about Pope Leo's letter, although Photius, for good reasons, never mentions it.

In the extant eighteen homilies of Photius there is only one reference to the procession of the Spirit, a reference which seems to presuppose the beginning of the controversy with the Franks. Homily XVI, according to Cyril Mango, was given on March 2, 867.[3] Photius states that the Father is the "cause of the Holy Ghost" and that the Spirit is not included in the birth of the Son just as the Son has no share in the procession of the Spirit.[4] There is nothing seriously polemical about this statement and it in no way implies that Photius had "sources" at his disposal concerning the Latin view of the *Filioque*. This statement presupposes only that Photius understood Greek triadology, had heard of the doctrine of the *Filioque*, and was intelligent enough to draw certain conclusions from the very idea of the Spirit's alleged procession from the Father and the Son.

Photius' Encyclical is of the same nature. From the very idea of the *Filioque doctrine* he is able to draw certain conclusions, conclusions which do not necessitate his having anything other than the idea of the *Filioque* itself.

But there is a remarkable change in Photius' methodology in his letter to the Patriarch of Aquileia and his *Mystagogia*.

---

[2]*The Homilies of Photius, Patriarch of Constantinople*, translation, introduction and commentary by Cyril Mango (Cambridge: Harvard University Press, 1958), p. 21f.

[3]*Ibid.*, p. 24.

[4]*Ibid.*, p. 276.

In these later two works he knows quite well the arguments which the Carolingians use to support the *Filioque doctrine* and its interpolation in the Ecumenical Creed. It is reasonable to conclude that the works of the Carolingian theologians supplied Photius with this knowledge. Pope Nicholas, in writing to Hincmar, asked Hincmar to enlist the support of the Carolingian theologians and Pope Nicholas explicitly states that when he has received these works, he will send them to Constantinople.

In his later two writings Photius is aware of the Carolingian appeal to the Bible and to the Church Fathers. He explicitly writes that the "fruits of your *studies*" are not good.[5]

As far as is historically known, there were only three Carolingian responses to Pope Nicholas' appeal. Aeneas of Paris, Ratramnus of Corbie, and the Council of Worms all fulfilled the papal request. It is possible that all three responses, along with other earlier Carolingian writings, were sent to Constantinople. This in no sense means that Photius read full Greek translations of these works. Most probably the Byzantines summarized the Carolingian works. But from the internal evidence of the content of Photius' letter to the Patriarch of Aquileia and his *Mystagogia* it seems reasonable to conclude, as does Hergenröther, that the work which really attracted the attention of Photius was Ratramnus'. The main reasons for so concluding follow.

First, there is no Carolingian work which stresses so constantly the Biblical fact that the Spirit is the Spirit "of the Son." In fact, Ratramnus essentially brings all his Biblical, patristic, and dialectical arguments back to the idea that the Spirit is "of the Son." In his letter to the Patriarch of Aquileia and in his *Mystagogia* Photius is pre-occupied with criticizing the argument that since the Spirit is the Spirit "of the Son," he therefore proceeds from the Son. The emphasis of this argument in Ratramnus and Photius' preoccupation with it seem to indicate that Photius had con-

---

[5]*PG* 102, 348

fronted in some form the work of Ratramnus. Photius was most concerned with this argument because the statement, the "Spirit of the Son," was an uncontested Biblical fact and a dominant theme in Greek patristic literature. Photius' objective is to show that the Latin interpretation has distorted the original meaning of the text.

Secondly, Ratramnus also deals at length with the Biblical statement that the Son has "all" that the Father has. Photius expends much energy in criticizing the Carolingian interpretation of this text, again indicating that Photius had in some way assimilated Ratramnus' arguments.

Thirdly, why is Photius so concerned with proving that the Roman Church has not *added* to the Creed and that the Roman Church is in agreement with the other Four Patriarchs on this issue? Why does Photius spend so much time in appealing to the Roman Popes, both past and present? If Photius had confronted the work of Ratramnus, then his appeal to papal authority stands out more clearly. Ratramnus' work is the only Carolingian work which claims that the *Filioque* was added to the Creed by the Roman Church. Furthermore, Ratramnus writes that "none are in communion with the Catholic Church while they separate themselves from communion with Rome."[6] Photius' methodology is concentrated on proving that it was not Rome which added to the Creed. Indirectly Photius reveals that, according to the argument of Ratramnus, it is the Carolingian West, not the Byzantines, who have separated themselves from "communion with the Catholic Church."

18) For Photius the Council of 879-880, as evidenced from his own testimony in his letter to the Patriarch of Aquileia and his *Mystagogia*, had paramount significance. In fact, the Council considered itself "Ecumenical." Photius considered the sixth session of this Council as the effective means of halting the interpolated Creed in the Latin West. And, to a certain extent, Photius' policy of alliance with

---

[6]*PL* 121, 271-272.

the Roman See did halt the spread of the interpolated Creed in the West. Rome reaffirmed its ancient policy of not altering the Creed but the Roman policy was not efficacious in curtailing the custom among the Germanic north.

It is noteworthy that Photius in principle was not opposed to "additions" to the Creed. In his statement about the Creed at the Council of 879-880 Photius allows for the possibility of adding to the Creed,[7] but only on the condition that such action is necessitated by a new heresy. It is assumed, of course, that any future addition to the Creed would have to be promulgated by an Ecumenical Council and be approved by the entire Church.

19) The intricacies of the Byzantine-Carolingian Triadological controversy and the extant historical information should cause one to be cautious about rejecting the authenticity of Pope John's letter to Photius. There is nothing in the content of the letter which is inconsistent with Roman policy at that time.

20) Photius' "ecumenical" spirit is at times ambiguous and inconsistent. In his second letter to Pope Nicholas he explicitly refers to the disciplinary differences between the Latin West and the Greek East, stating that the canons of the Quinisext Council do not in fact apply to the Western Church. In his Encyclical, however, he wants the canons of the Quinisext Council to be applied universally.

On the one hand, Photius' "ecumenical" spirit causes him to work out a *theology of the Fathers* which specifically protects the Latin Fathers who taught the *Filioque*. On the other hand, Photius has contempt for the Latin language itself.

But it is strikingly clear that Photius does not really consider the disciplinary differences between the Latin West and the Greek East as that serious. Even in his Encyclical his primary concern is with the *Filioque*. The proof that

---

[7]Mansi 17, 516; lines 33-35.

Conclusions 173

Photius considered the *Filioque* addition to the Creed as the only serious problem between the Greek East and the Frankish West is the fact that later all his energies are devoted not to disciplinary problems but to the problem of the *Filioque*. Photius' main objective was the restoration of peace and doctrinal unity in the Church.

21) Although Photius often appeals to the authority of the statement ascribed to Christ in John 15:26 ["who proceeds from the Father..."], he never specifically points out the rather ironic fact that there was only *one* expression in the Ecumenical Creed which, according to the Gospel of John, was Christ's own statement. Ironically, it was only this one expression which was altered.

22) It is noteworthy that Photius sought conciliar action —as far as is known—only on the problem of the addition of the *Filioque* to the Creed. He did not seek conciliar discussion of and condemnation of the *doctrine* of the *Filioque* itself, except implicitly, even though he considered the doctrine as "blasphemously" wrong.

The wisest step for the ultimate unity of the Church which Photius could have taken was to have initiated "Ecumenical" discussions on the Latin interpretation of the *Filioque* doctrine. Although Photius obviously thought that the delicate political and ecclesiastical situation at that time rendered such a step impossible, he may have misread the spirit of the time. Historically his greatest mistake was in underestimating the seriousness and the potential influence of the Germanic north. If his "ecumenical" spirit had been more "universal," an Ecumenical Council might have been convoked, including Frankish representatives. This would have brought the entire problem, both as an interpolation of the Creed and as *doctrine*, before the entire Church for open discussion. If Photius had energetically pursued such a policy, it is possible that some solution of the entire problem might have been reached. Indeed, Photius knew quite well what was needed in solving the problems of discord in the Church, for in his second letter to Pope Nicholas he wrote:

> In reality nothing is more exalted and more precious than love.... Through love those who are separated are united.... Through love the inner ecumenical bonds are more firmly knitted together; [through love] the entrance of discord and jealousy is shut off . . . because love thinks no evil, it cherishes all things, it hopes all things, it endures all things and love never fades.... And for those who share the same religion, even though they live so far apart, even though they have never seen each other face to face, love binds them in unity and unites them in the same conviction...[8]

This was the only opportune time in the history of the Church when the problem could have been discussed fruitfully. But, unfortunately, the decisive moment in the history of the Church was not acted upon.

Theological Conclusions

"To his Biblical, patristic, papal and conciliar argumentation [Photius] added a most impressive series of dialectical arguments."[9] Essentially Photius' dialectical methodology analyzes the doctrine of the *Filioque* from every perspective and, using the argument *ad absurdum*, reveals the logical inconsistencies and the logical conclusions which result from such a vision of the Godhead.

From within the framework of the Greek triadological "model" there is no place for the Latin interpretation of the *Filioque*, especially as expressed by the Carolingians.

For the Carolingians, the first principle of the Godhead is the Divine Essence. For Photius, the first principle of the Godhead is God the Father. According to Photius' triadological "model," there is no way that the Spirit can derive his existence from the Son without radically undermining or destroying the Divine Triad. For the Carolingians, pro-

---

[8]*PG* 102, 593f.

[9]Edmund J. Fortman, *The Triune God* (Philadelphia: Westminster Press, 1972), p. 94.

Conclusions

cession is ultimately a result of the Divine Essence. For Photius, procession is personal; all that is common in the Godhead belongs to the Divine Essence. The Divine Persons, for Photius, are, by definition and through revealed truth, precisely not common; hence, they cannot proceed or come forth from the Divine Essence.

According to Photius, if procession is the result of the Divine Essence, then the Holy Spirit must proceed from himself, the Father must also have a procession, and the Son must either come forth from himself or from the Father and the Spirit.

For Photius, the *Filioque* doctrine splits the Divine Triad into either a Dyad or a Tetrad. Dyadic, if the Father and the Son produce the Spirit in a common act of love from which the Spirit is excluded. Tetradic, if the Three Persons "come forth" from the first principle which is the Divine Essence. Photius also maintains that the inner logics of the *Filioque* doctrine lead to polytheism. According to Photius, in producing the Spirit the Father shares his unique, personal attribute with the Son, causing the oneness of the Father and the oneness of the Son to be divided. Hence, the Spirit is also divided, the result of which are six divisions within the Godhead.

For Photius, the *Filioque* doctrine implied that the Spirit was further removed from the Father than was the Son and hence the Spirit was relegated to an inferior rank. In what sense, according to Photius, could the equality of the Divine Persons be maintained, if the Son is given the "honor" of being a cause of another Divine Person? Should not the Spirit, then, also be given the "honor" of being a cause of the Son?

And Photius cannot see what the Spirit gains in his alleged procession from the Son. Is not God the Father perfect? If he is perfect, then the procession of the Spirit from the Father is perfect and a procession from the Son would be existentially superfluous.

Photius' triadology was not the last word of Eastern Christianity on the procession of the Spirit. Indeed, in struggling to oppose the *Filioque* doctrine, Photius failed to consider the various interpretations of the Greek patristic idea of the procession of the Spirit through the Son. For Photius, the "διὰ τοῦ Υἱοῦ" referred only to the "economic" activity of the Holy Trinity; that is, the Spirit's procession *through* the Son was restricted to the Spirit's temporal mission. For Photius there seems to be no room for a procession through the Son in the eternal, inner life of the Holy Trinity. Because of this the Photian triadological scheme has often been accused of neglecting an eternal relationship between the Son and the Spirit. Although these accusations may be somewhat just, nevertheless these conclusions do not necessarily follow from Photius' *basic* triadological vision.

The Holy Spirit can be said to proceed eternally from the Father through the Son without implying that the Spirit takes his existence from the Son. If one takes seriously the Biblical and patristic vision of the Spirit proceeding from the Father through the Son, or proceeding from the Father together with the Son and remaining on and in the Son, and dependent on the Son, then an eternal relationship between the Son and the Spirit is mandatory. But this eternal relationship does not have to be existential. There can be eternal relations in the life of the Holy Trinity which are not existentially *causal* relations.

For example, the Causing-Father relates causally, as Cause, to the Un-Causing Son. And the Caused and Un-Causing Son relates eternally, dynamically, responsively, and *uncausally,* to the Causing-Father. If, therefore, the Un-Causing Son can relate to the Father eternally, why can there not be an eternal relationship between the Un-Causing Son and the Un-Causing Spirit?

From within the basic framework of the Greek triadological "model" the Augustinian idea of the Spirit being the love of the Father and the Son can be interpreted without implying the Spirit's procession from the Son. In fact, according to Photius, the Latin view of the Spirit being the result of the love between the Father and the Son is defective. For the Latin triadological "model" the Father and

Conclusions 177

the Son are united in reciprocal love, the result of which is the passive procession of the Holy Spirit. The Latin view is adequately expressed by Paul Henry.

> It is generally agreed that the Spirit is the mutual Love of Father and Son. But this statement is often (and falsely) taken to imply that the Spirit unites the first two Persons.... He is thought to be the bond between Father and Son, the means by which they love one another. That is not the case. He is the expression, the fruit, the result of their love and unity.[10]

According to Photius, the Latin view implies that the Spirit is excluded from the very act of love.

From within the general framework of the Greek triadological "model" the Father begets his Son whom he loves and this love, the Holy Spirit, simultaneously proceeds, or springs forth, from the Father to embrace the Son. The Son, loving the Father in return, embraces the Father also. Hence, according to this scheme, the Holy Spirit, proceeds eternally from the Father to the Son and through the Son to the Father. According to this idea, the Holy Spirit is not the result of the love between the Father and the Son but is rather the very hypostatic love of the Father for the Son and the Son for the Father.

From within this perspective it is possible to say that the Holy Spirit proceeds from the Father and the Son, *provided that it is understood that the Spirit does not take his very existence from the Son*. But this is, of course, the essence of the controversy between the Greek East and the Latin West.

---

[10]Paul Henry, "On Some Implications of the '*Ex Patre Filioque Tanquam Ab Uno Principio*'," *Eastern Churches Quarterly*, VII, 2 (1948), 21.

APPENDIX

The Patristic Background

In their attack on Byzantine Triadology the Carolingian theologians constantly appeal to the "authority" of the Church Fathers to support their position that the Holy Spirit proceeds; that is, derives his very existence, from both the Father and the Son. Although the most authoritative and most important Church Father for the Carolingian theologians is Augustine, they also appeal to Athanasius, Didymus the Blind, Gregory of Nazianzus, Cyril of Alexandria, Hilary, Ambrose, and numerous post-Augustinian Latin theologians. The primary focus of this appendix is only on those "patristic authorities" to whom the Carolingians appeal. Only Cyril of Alexandria and Augustine are studied in depth and I am gratefully indebted to Professor Serge Verhovskoy for many of the insights.

I

INTRODUCTORY BACKGROUND

The Apologists were primarily concerned with the work

of the Holy Spirit rather than with the Spirit's eternal relation to the Father and the Son. This tendency to avoid the inner existence of the Holy Trinity[1] resulted in an ambiguity which has caused the Apologists to be suspected of subordinationism; that is, that there is no real equality among the Persons, that "God" is truly the Father, and the Son and the Spirit are intermediaries between the Father and the world. This tendency appears one-sided and prepared the way for later subordinationists. However, it is difficult to prove that the Apologists' one-sided emphasis on the Trinity in relation to the world is, in fact, real subordinationism.[2] It is just as valid to interpret their thought as stressing the idea that God the Father is absolutely transcendent and hence is related to the world through his Son and his Spirit.

Another tendency, the opposite of subordinationism, came to be known as Modalism and later as Sabellianism. For the Modalists and Sabellians God was essentially a monad who expressed himself in different modes at different times. Modalism was actually an early form of Unitarianism, for its tendency was to undermine the reality of the Divine Persons. In fact, because it was claimed to obliterate the distinction between the Father and the Son, it was later referred to as the υἱοπάτωρ heresy, a term the Christian East would later use in reference to the Latin doctrine of the *Filioque*.

---

[1]Theophilus of Antioch was the first to use the Greek term Τριάς c. 180 (in *Ad Autolycum* II, 15), albeit in the strange sequence of God, His Logos, and His Wisdom. Tertullian was the first to use the Latin term *trinitas* c. 213 (in *Adversus Praxeam*).

[2]For example, Origen's. It is noteworthy that Régnon, following the testimony of Athanasius, acquits Origen of subordinationism. (See Théodore de Régnon, *Études de Théologie positive sur La Sainte Trinité*, troisième série (Paris, 1898), p. 8). Although it is true that Origen in his *De Principiis* 1, 2, 4 claims, in an almost anti-Arian statement, that there was no time when the Son was not, there are numerous statements and lines of thought in Origen which clearly imply subordinationism. Concerning the procession of the Holy Spirit, it is noteworthy that Origen seems to approach the later Latin view in his *Commentary on the Epistle to the Romans*. (See *PG* 14, 1098).

Tertullian's *Adversus Praxeam* was written against one of the early Modalists. According to H. B. Swete, Tertullian was the "first to formulate the floating belief of the Church as to the Divine Processions and . . . in his writings we also find the first distinct approximation to the Western doctrine of the Procession of the Holy Ghost."[3] This statement, however, seems to be an exaggeration, prompted by Tertullian's suggestive analogy that the "Spirit is third from God and the Son, just as the fruit from the branch is third from the root, and as the stream from the river is third from the spring, and as the light from the ray is third from the sun."[4] Although this analogy could be interpreted within the perspective of the *Filioque* doctrine, it can also be interpreted within the perspective of the *per Filium* teaching. Indeed, it is difficult to find anything in Tertullian which goes beyond a *per Filium* teaching. In fact, while assuring Praxeas that it is impossible to destroy the "monarchy" in the Trinity, Tertullian explicitly states that the Spirit proceeds from the Father through the Son.[5]

An accurate assessment of Christian thought on the procession of the Spirit before the Arian crisis follows:

> . . . the elements of the controversy have been seen to be already at work. The Church had begun to seek an answer to the question, 'Whence is the Spirit of God and of Christ? how is He related to the Father? how to the Son?' Already from North Africa and Alexandria the answer has been substantially given, 'He is from the Father; He is through the Son.' But no Church, no individual teacher has yet ventured to say 'He is from Both.'[6]

---

[3]H.B. Swete, *On the History of the Doctrine of the Procession of the Holy Spirit* (London, 1876), p. 54.

[4]Tertullian, *Adversus Praxeam* 8.

[5]Tertullian, *Adversus Praxeam* 4 (PL 2, 159).

[6]Swete, *op. cit.*, p. 73.

II

THE GREEK PATRISTIC BACKGROUND

Athanasius

Arianism denied that the Son is eternally begotten from the Father as true God from true God. Hence, the Church's opposition to Arianism stressed the consubstantiality of the essence of the Divine Persons. Arianism, although defeated in the Greek East, lingered on in the Latin West through the Arianism of various Germanic tribes. Hence, Arianism in various forms became a crucial problem for the Latin "Catholic" West, especially in Spain, and was never forgotten by the Carolingian theologians. The Latin West constantly invoked the name of Athanasius against the Arianism of the Germanic tribes.

Athanasius (c. 295-373) was primarily concerned with the Divinity, rather than the origin, of the Holy Spirit. To prove the Divinity of the Spirit, he stresses the inseparability of the Spirit from the Son.[7] Because of this stress, Athanasius' scheme of the Trinity becomes linear; that is, he forms an analogy between the Father and Son and the Son and the Spirit. This linear scheme is often interpreted to support the later Latin doctrine of the procession of the Spirit from the Son. But in his authentic works "he nowhere states explicitly that the Holy Spirit proceeds from the Son...."[8]

Athanasius does, however, state that if the Son belongs to the essence of the Father[9] because he is ἐκ τοῦ Πατρός,

---

[7]See *Contra Arianos* 3; *Epistula ad Serapionem* I, 16, 20, 25; IV, 3.

[8]Johannes Quasten, *Patrology* (3 vols.: Westminster: Newman Press, 1950-1960), III, 77.

[9]*Ad Serapionem* I, 25: "Ἴδιος τῆς οὐσίας τοῦ Πατρός."

then the Spirit belongs to the essence of the Son[10] because he is ἐκ τοῦ Θεοῦ. Although some see in Athanasius' linear scheme an implicit adumbration of the later Latin doctrine of the *Filioque*, it is clear that Athanasius' triadological thought lends itself to another interpretation.

In the New Testament and in Greek patristic thought the term ὁ Θεὸς refers to God the Father, while the word without the article refers to the Divine Being as such. Hence, when Athanasius uses the expression ἐκ τοῦ Θεοῦ, it is a reference to God the Father. God is identified as God the Father and, consequently, possessing the essence from the Father means to be God.

Athanasius claims it is impossible to be the Spirit without being the Spirit of someone.[11] Since the Spirit is the Spirit of the Son, he is therefore God.[12] Athanasius, as other Greek patristic writers, sees a monarchistic principle [μοναρχία] in the Holy Trinity: God the Father is the unique principle and source.[13] The Holy Spirit proceeds from the Father, although he belongs to the Son and is given to mankind by the Son.[14] The Holy Spirit is neither the Son of God nor the Son of the Son.[15] He is from God and is in God.[16] Since the Son is the Wisdom, the Truth, and the Power of the Father, and since the Spirit is the Spirit of the Son, he is therefore the Spirit of Wisdom, Truth, and Power.[17] The Holy Spirit is therefore the Image of the Son.[18] But, and quite importantly, if the Holy Spirit is the Image of the Son, the Son is the Image of the Father, and therefore the Father is

---

[10]*Ibid.*: "ἴδιον κατ' οὐσίαν τοῦ Υἱοῦ."

[11]*Ad Serapionem* I, 4, 25.

[12]*Contra Arianos* 4, 1.

[13]*Ad Serapionem* I, 19 and 20.

[14]*Ibid.*, II, 11.

[15]*Ibid.*, I, 11.

[16]*Ibid.*, I, 21, 25, 25; IV, 4.

[17]*Ibid.*, I, 25.

[18]*Ibid.*, I, 24; IV, 3.

the prototype of both. The Son abides in the Spirit.[19] The Holy Spirit is the perfect, holy, illuminating Energy and Gift of the Son. This Energy proceeds from the Father but it shines from, is sent by, and is given from the Son, who is from the Father.[20]

This inseparability is stressed again and again. The Source of everything is the Father but, because of Athanasius' linear scheme, the Son is seen as an eternal "intermediary" between the Father and the Spirit.[21] Thus, the procession of the Spirit is from the Father through the Son.

Athanasius' vision of the personal or hypostatic life of God is quite realistic. Persons are not merely relations of origin; they are real.

> It is a Triad not only in name and form of speech, but in truth and actuality. For as the Father is He who is, so also His word is one who is and God over all. And the Holy Spirit is not without actual existence, but exists and has true being. Less than these [Persons] the Catholic Church does not hold, lest she sink to the level of the modern Jews . . . and to the level of Sabellius.[22]

In Athanasius' triadology there is no notion of a Spirator. The Holy Spirit proceeds from the Father;[23] he depends on and is, of course, inseparable from the Son, but he does not proceed *as existing* from the Son.

If, however, one already has assimilated the Latin teaching of the procession of the Spirit from the Father and the Son, then it is not difficult to interpret the triadology of Athanasius in that direction.

Historically, the real problem arose with the pseudo-Athanasian corpus, works which the Latin West sincerely thought were written by Athanasius. The pseudo-Athanasian

---

[19]*Ibid.*, I, 20.

[20]*Ibid.*

[21]*Contra Arianos* 3, 24-25.

[22]*Ad Serapionem* I, 28. (The English translation is from *The Letters of Saint Athanasius Concerning the Holy Spirit*, trans. by C.R.B. Shapland (New York, 1951), p. 135 f.).

[23]*Ibid.*, I, 2.

corpus includes the *De incarnatione contra Apollinarem*,[24] the *Sermo maior de fide*,[25] the *Expositio fidei*,[26] the *Interpretatio in symbolum*,[27] the *Dialogi contra Macedonianos*,[28] the *Dialogi de sancta Trinitate quinque*,[29] the *De Trinitate Libri XII*,[30] and the remarkably influential *Symbolum Athanasianum*. Indeed, there can be no question that the *Filioque* doctrine is taught in these spurius works.

It is quite possible that Marcellus of Ancyra (d. 374)[31] wrote the *Sermo maior de fide* and the *Expositio fidei* and that Didymus the Blind (313-398)[32] authored the *Dialogi de sancta Trinitate*. The *De Trinitate Libri XII* "represent a collection of treatises by several unknown authors of the West, who composed them approximately in the second half of the fourth and in the fifth century."[33] Parts of the *De Trinitate Libri XII* were used by both Ambrose and Augustine. The origin of the incalculably influential *Symbolum Athanasianum* was treated in Chapter II of this study.

Thus, as a result of a later, perhaps one-sided, interpretation of his authentic works and a correct interpretation of the spurius works under his name, Athanasius became one of the most authoritative of the Greek Fathers for the Carolingian theologians, who had no way of knowing that most of the works they appealed to were spurious.

---

[24]*PG* 26, 1093-1166.

[25]*PG* 26, 1263-1294.

[26]*PG* 25, 199-208.

[27]*PG* 26, 1231-1232.

[28]*PG* 28, 1291-1338.

[29]*PG* 28, 1115-1286.

[30]*PL* 62, 237-334.

[31]See F. Scheidweiler, "Wer ist der Verfasser des sogenannten Sermo maior de fide?" *Byzantinische Zeitschrift*, XLVII (1954), 333-357. It appears from Eusebius of Caesarea's *De ecclesiastica theologia* (*PG* 24, 1013), an attack on Marcellus which quotes from Marcellus, that the latter comes quite close to the later Latin doctrine of the *Filioque*.

[32]See A. Günthör, *Die sieben pseudo-athanasianischen Dialoge, ein Werk Didymus des Blinden* (Rome, 1941).

[33]Quasten, *op. cit.*, III, 33-34.

Didymus the Blind

Two important works by Didymus the Blind on the Trinity are extant; however, only his *De Trinitate* is extant in the original Greek. The other work, *De Spiritu Sancto*, has survived only in the questionable Latin translation by Jerome.

In his *De Trinitate* Didymus interprets St. Paul's "the Spirit of God" as the Spirit who proceeds from the Person of God.[34] The eternal procession of the Spirit from the Father and the eternal begetting of the Son from the Father are co-eternal and parallel acts.[35] The Spirit proceeds from the Father and, of course, remains in the Son.[36] In his *De Trinitate* Didymus teaches the common Greek patristic view of the procession of the Spirit from the Father through the Son.

However, in the extant Latin translation of *De Spiritu Sancto*, a translation for which "there is reason to fear that later hands have tampered with,"[37] there is definitely a teaching of the procession of the Spirit from the Father and the Son.

> In operation the Spirit is one with the Father and the Son, and this oneness of operation involves oneness of essence. He is the Father of God; the Seal which stamps the Divine image on the human soul. But He is not merely an operating force; He is a Divine Person. He goes forth from the Father,[38] He is sent by the Son, not as angels or prophets are sent, but as indivisibly one with the Person who sent Him . . . Our Lord teaches that the being

---

[34] *De Trinitate* II, 2 (*PG* 39, 456): "Τὸ ἐκ τοῦ Θεοῦ τῆς ὑποστάσεως ἐκπορευθέν."

[35] *PG* 39, 460.

[36] *PG* 39, 426.

[37] Swete, *op. cit.*, p. 94. Quasten also questions whether "the Latin translation of St. Jerome does justice to the original" on this very matter. See Quasten, *op. cit.*, p. 96.

[38] It is noteworthy that Martin Jugie in his *De Processione Spiritus Sancti* (Rome, 1936), p. 136 omits this part of the text.

The Patristic Background

of the Spirit is derived not from the Spirit Himself, but from the Father and the Son; He goes forth from the Son, proceeding from the Truth; He has no substance but that which is given Him by the Son.[39]

There can be no doubt that this is clearly the view which the Latin West will later accept. Whether it is actually the teaching of Didymus or an addition by Jerome remains uncertain. However, the historical importance of this text lies in the fact that it was in this form that it reached the Latin West and provided the Carolingians with a "Greek" patristic authority to support their position.

The Cappadocian Fathers

For the Cappadocian Fathers—Basil the Great (d. 364), Gregory of Nazianzus (d. 389), and Gregory of Nyssa (d. 394)—God the Father is the source of all existence.[40] The Son and the Holy Spirit come forth from the Father.[41] The Holy Spirit is inseparable from the Son[42] and, in fact, the very existence of the Son cannot even be conceived without the existence of the Spirit.[43]

The Cappadocian Fathers stress the reality of the personal existence in God and establish their thought of personal

---

[39]The English translation is from H.B. Swete, *The Holy Spirit in the Ancient Church* (London, 1912), p. 224.

[40]See Basil, *De Spiritu Sancto* 18, 46; the authentic books of his *Adversus Eunomium; Epistola* 52 and *Epistola* 38, 3 [which, according to A. Cavallin's *Studien zu den Briefen des heiligen Basilius* (Lund, 1944) is spurious]; Gregory of Nazianzus, *Oratio* 20, 10-11; 25, 15-16; 34, 10; 36, 10; 42; and Gregory of Nyssa, *Ad Graecos ex communibus notionibus*.

[41]See Gregory of Nazianzus, *Oratio* 29, 2; 42, 15; and Gregory of Nyssa, *Adversus Eunomium* I; *Quod non sint tres dii*.

[42]See Basil, *De Spiritu Sancto* 18, 46; Gregory of Nazianzus, *Oratio* 25, 16; 29, 13; and Gregory of Nyssa, *Oratio catechetica magna* 2.

[43]Gregory of Nyssa, *Adversus Eunomium* I.

life in God the Father, who is "Person." The Son and the Spirit are "Persons" because God the Father, from whom they come forth, is "Person." In order to be fully God, in order to possess the fulness of Divine Life, the Son and the Spirit must be "Persons." While seeing a difference in the "Persons" because of their relations, the Cappadocians never identify the relations, or for that matter any other characteristic of the "Person," with the "Person" itself. The "Persons" are real; they exist not just in relation to each other, but first of all they exist in themselves.

"St. Basil manifestly holds the common view of most of the Greek Fathers that the Holy Spirit proceeds from the Father through the Son."[44] Basil teaches "very distinctly and repeatedly that the Spirit is ἐκ Θεοῦ δι' Υἱοῦ ... Basil never suffers himself to pass from δι' Υἱοῦ into the ἐκ Υἱοῦ."[45] Nevertheless, there is a textual problem with the extant text of Basil's *Adversus Eunomium*. It is stated that the Spirit comes "after the Son because he takes his being from him."[46] This text was rejected by the Greeks at the Council of Florence as a later interpolation. It is commonly admitted that Basil's *Adversus Eunomium* has been tampered with; in fact, books IV and V were not written by Basil.[47] If the text is authentic and is interpreted within a pro-*Filioque* perspective, then the text is inconsistent with the totality of Basil's triadology.

In a much disputed text from the third Oration of Gregory of Nyssa's *De oratione dominica* one reads that "the Holy Spirit is also said to be from the Father, and is

---

[44]Quasten, *op. cit.*, III, 233.

[45]Swete, *On the History of the Doctrine of the Procession of the Holy Spirit*, p. 101.

[46]Basil, *Adversus Eunomium* III, 1 (*PG* 29, 656).

[47]See Quasten, *op .cit.*, III, 210. It is possible that Didymus authored these two books. If this is correct, then the above-mentioned text from Didymus' *De Spiritu Sancto* becomes more suspect of interpolation because book V of *Adversus Eunomium* is quite clear about the procession of the Spirit from the Father through the Son.

testified to be from [ἐκ] the Son."⁴⁸ The authenticity of this text has not been contested except for the preposition "from" [ἐκ] which is not found in many old manuscripts. But, even if the expression ἐκ τοῦ Υἱοῦ is Gregory's, "the words must be interpreted by his own fuller formula."⁴⁹

Although the Carolingian theologians, especially Ratramnus of Corbie, appeal to the authority of Gregory of Nazianzus, there is nothing in the triadological thought of Gregory which goes beyond the teaching of the procession of the Spirit from the Father through the Son.

Cyril of Alexandria

Cyril's (d. 444) triadological master is Athanasius on whom he relies extensively.⁵⁰ Cyril's triadological thought is not always clear because it suffers from a lack of precision in distinguishing between *nature* and *person,* the same problem which presents itself in Cyril's Christology. Two problems chiefly concern Cyril: (1) the Divinity of the Holy Spirit; and (2) the Spirit's belonging *by nature* to the Son of God.

If the Son of God is eternally God, then he must possess the Holy Spirit by nature. If the Holy Spirit can divinize and sanctify mankind, then he must be Divine. Cyril insists that the Holy Spirit is consubstantial with both the Father and the Son.⁵¹

---

⁴⁸A. Mai, *Nova Patrum Bibliotheca* IV (Rome, 1883), p. 53: "Τὸ δὲ Ἅγιον Πνεῦμα καὶ ἐκ τοῦ Πατρὸς λέγεται καὶ (ἐκ) τοῦ Υἱοῦ εἶναι προσμαρτυρεῖται.

⁴⁹Swete, *op. cit.,* p. 104. Swete also writes: "Judging from internal evidence it is difficult to believe that S. Gregory wrote the suspected preposition. Even Petavius saw and admitted that the context required its omission." *Ibid.*

⁵⁰For example, approximately a third of Cyril's *Thesaurus de sancta et consubstantiali Trinitate* is a reproduction of Athanasius' *Contra Arianos* III.

⁵¹See *Thesaurus* 3 (*PG* 75, 571, 576); 34 (PG 75, 585); and *De sancta et consubstantiali Trinitate* (PG 75, 1089 and 1129).

Cyril considers the Biblical names of Father, Son and Holy Spirit quite realistically. If the Father is really the Father and the Son is really the Son, then the Holy Spirit is really Holy. He is the personal Holiness who proceeds from the Father.[52] Although all the Divine Persons are Holy by nature, Holiness belongs to the Holy Spirit personally.

Cyril's language is ambiguous because sometimes he speaks as though he identifies the Holy Spirit with the Divine essence without distinguishing what is "natural" in God and what is "personal" or "hypostatic."[53] It becomes clear, however, that for Cyril, first of all, the Father possesses or has his Son and the Son is in the Father. Secondly, the Holy Spirit belongs necessarily to the Father. Since the Father has the Spirit, and since the Father gives everything to the Son, then the Father gives the Spirit to the Son. The real point is that the Spirit is "given" by the Father. If the Spirit proceeds from the Son, then there would be no meaning to the "giving."

The Holy Spirit belongs to the Son. In fact, their relations are so close that it is impossible to say that the Son, acting by or in the Holy Spirit, acts by himself.[54] Cyril almost identifies them; he sees, of course, the cause of this proximity in the consubstantiality of the Holy Spirit, who belongs to the Son naturally and substantially. Cyril establishes a suggestive analogy: as the finger naturally belongs to the hand, so the Holy Spirit is united to the Son consubstantially, although he proceeds from the Father.[55] Since the Holy Spirit belongs to the Son, he is in the Son, by him, and from him.[56] The Holy Spirit is the "radiance" of the Word of God, shining by the light of his own hypostasis or person.[57]

---

[52]*Thesaurus* 33 (*PG* 75, 579).

[53]See Cyril's *Commentary on John* (*PG* 74, 540-541).

[54]*Ibid.* (*PG* 74, 548 and 549).

[55]See Cyril's *Commentary on Luke* (*PG* 72, 704).

[56]*Commentary on John* (*PG* 73, 753).

[57]*Ibid.* (*PG* 74, 545).

There are times when Cyril writes that the Holy Spirit proceeds "from the substance of the Son,"[58] or that he springs from the Divine nature.[59] The Spirit is of the Divine essence and proceeds substantially from it and in it.[60] But if Cyril means that the Holy Spirit proceeds as Person from his own essence, then an obvious contradiction arises. It must be stressed that Cyril's main concern is to show that Christ must possess the Holy Spirit by nature if both Christ and the Holy Spirit are divine. Cyril ignores the implications of his ambiguous language.

Although Cyril states that the Holy Trinity is involved in every action, he maintains that the Father is the source of the action and that the Son accomplishes the work in the Holy Spirit.[61]

Is Cyril a partisan of the later Latin interpretation of the *Filioque*? Hubert du Manoir de Juaye is quite correct when he remarks that "Cyril of Alexandria has been considered as one of the most authoritative defenders of the *Filioque* . . . Catholic polemicists . . . who were forced to refute the theories of Photius, frequently cite Cyril and take a certain number of texts which favor the Roman position."[62] The real issues of the interpretation which seeks to make Cyril a partisan of the Latin interpretation of the *Filioque* seem to be the following: (1) If the Holy Spirit belongs to the Son, then, it is claimed, Christ's influence cannot be exercised unless the Holy Spirit proceeds from him; (2) If the Spirit depends on the Son, he ought also to depend on the Son for his very existence; (3) If the Son is the image of the Father and proceeds from him, then, if the Spirit is the image of the Son, he ought to proceed from the Son;

---

[58]*Ibid.* (*PG* 74, 444).

[59]*Ibid.* (*PG* 74, 257).

[60]*Thesaurus* 34 (*PG* 75, 585).

[61]See Cyril's *Adversus Nestorii* (*PG* 76, 172 and 180); *Commentary on John* (*PG* 74, 541).

[62]Hubert du Manoir de Juaye, S. J., *Dogme et Spiritualité chez Saint Cyrille d'Alexandrie* (Paris, 1944), p. 225.

(4) If the Spirit is the Spirit "of the Son," then he ought to proceed from the Son; and (5) If the Spirit proceeds from the Divine nature, then he ought also to proceed from the Son because the Son shares the divine nature with the Father.

In response to the above interpretation it must be admitted, first of all, that logically influence has nothing to do with origin. Secondly, dependence and source are not logically related. Thirdly, the Holy Spirit is the image of the Son but the Son is the image of the Father; therefore, the ultimate source of the image is the Father. Fourthly, as Photius later observes, to be "of" does not mean "to proceed eternally from." And fifthly, if the Holy Spirit proceeds from the Divine Nature, then he proceeds from himself.

But the problem can be placed in a broader perspective. If the Spirit is considered as an intermediary between the Father and the Son, and if the Spirit is in the Son, it is logical to arrive at the doctrine of the procession of the Spirit from the Father through the Son. But the real problem lies in the interpretation of "through the Son."

There are many texts which show that Cyril did not believe that the Spirit derived his very existence from the Son.[63] The problem is that Cyril unites his teaching with the essence of God.[64] In his *Commentary on John* Cyril states that the Holy Spirit is given to creatures by the Son because the Son in his nature is from the Father and in the Father and he possesses the Holy Spirit who "belongs" to the nature of the Father and flows out from the Father through the Word, who is consubstantial with the Father.[65] The Holy Spirit is from the Father and from the Son *essentially;* that is, he is consubstantial with them, but he flows out of the Father through the Son.[66] It is noteworthy that Cyril reasons

---

[63]*Commentary on John* (*PG* 73, 753; *PG* 74, 170, 444, 449, 542, 709).

[64]*De sancta et consubstantiali Trinitate* (*PG* 75, 1009).

[65]*Commentary on John* (*PG* 74, 540).

[66]*De adoratione et cultu in spiritu et veritate* (*PG* 68, 148).

from the opposite direction also: if the Spirit is through the Son, then he must be consubstantial with him.[67]

Another problem is that Cyril often speaks of the procession (using several Greek words for procession) of the Spirit without clarifying whether it is an eternal procession or a temporal mission.

Cyril writes that the Spirit proceeds naturally or substantially in the Son.[68] Cyril believes that the Holy Spirit proceeds from the Father, but since the Holy Trinity is One, the Holy Spirit cannot be separated from the Son. The problem, if there is one, is in explaining the dependence of the Spirit on the Son from a trinitarian perspective. There seems, however, to be an answer. The Son is the personal or hypostatic Wisdom of the Father and the Holy Spirit is the Life and Perfection of the fulness of God. Thus, if the Son is the personal Truth of the Father, and if the Spirit is the Spirit of Truth and Wisdom, then he is "from" the Son in the sense of proceeding "through" the Son. Thus the Holy Spirit proceeds directly from the Father, remains in the Son, receives from the Son everything which belongs to the Son, and then manifests them in and by his own person.

The historical proof that Cyril did not regard the Son as the existential source of the Spirit is Cyril's encounter with the Church of Antioch. In his synodical letter to Nestorius Cyril wrote that the Spirit is "from God and the Father."[69] In his ninth anathema Cyril wrote that the Holy Spirit was Christ's own Spirit.[70] Theodoret of Cyrus (d. 466) responded rather sharply on behalf of the Church of Antioch:

> That the Spirit is the Son's very own, of the same nature with him and proceeding from the Father, we admit and accept as pious truth; but if Cyril means that the Spirit has His subsistence from or through the Son, we reject this as blasphemous and impious.[71]

---

[67]*Commentary on John* (PG 74, 552).
[68]*Thesaurus* (PG 75, 576 and 571).
[69]PG 77, 117.
[70]PG 77, 121.
[71]PG 76, 432.

Cyril clarified his position in his response to Theodoret:

> The Spirit was and is the Son's as He was and is the Father's; for though He proceeds from the Father, yet He is not alien from the Son; for the Son has all things in common with the Father, as the Lord has Himself taught us.[72]

Swete writes that "it is evident that Cyril would have been ready to accept the formula *ex utroque*, provided that it was explained to mean *ex Patre per filium*."[73]

Nevertheless, it is quite easy to see how Cyril's statements could later be used by the Carolingian theologians in an attempt to find "Greek patristic" authority to support their interpretation of the procession of the Spirit from the Father and the Son. Their interpretation of Cyril's triadology may not be correct, but it is historically quite understandable.

III

THE LATIN PATRISTIC BACKGROUND

Hilary of Poitiers

Turning from the Greek patristic East to the Latin patristic West, one finds that the question of the procession of the Spirit was already quite controversial in Gaul, in Italy, and in North Africa. There were those who claimed that the Spirit proceeded from the Father alone, those who maintained that he proceeded from the Father and the Son, and others who believed he proceeded from the Father through the Son.

In his *De Trinitate* Hilary of Poitiers (c. 315-c. 367)

---

[72] *PG* 76, 433.

[73] H. B. Swete, *The Holy Spirit in the Ancient Church* (London, 1912), p. 269.

attests to this controversy, writing that "for the present I forbear to expose *their* license of speculation, some of them holding that the Paraclete Spirit comes from the Father or from the Son."[74] In his concluding prayer to God the Father Hilary clearly states his belief in the procession of the Spirit from the Father through the Son.

> But, for my part, I cannot be content by the service of my faith and voice, to deny that my Lord and my God, Thy Only-Begotten, Jesus Christ, is a creature; I must also deny that this name of 'creature' belongs to the Holy Spirit, *seeing that He proceeds from Thee* and is *sent through Him* . . . so I hold fast in my consciousness the truth that thy Holy Spirit is *from Thee and through Him*, although I cannot by my intellect comprehend it . . . Keep, I pray Thee, this my pious faith undefiled, and even until my spirit departs, grant that this may be the utterance of my convictions . . . Let me, in short, adore Thee our Father, and Thy Son together with Thee; let me win the favour of Thy Holy Spirit, who is *from Thee, through thy Only-Begotten*.[75]

Ambrose

Quite often Ambrose (d. 397) uses the traditional Greek patristic teaching of the procession of the Spirit from the Father through the Son. At other times he uses the expression "from the Father and the Son" or "from the Son." However, in each case the topic under discussion is the temporal mission of the Holy Spirit.[76] "It can hardly be said that in the genuine works of S. Ambrose the phrase *procedere ex (a) Filio* is used with direct reference to an eternal ἐκπό-

---

[74]*De Trinitate* VIII, 20 (*PL* 10, 250). (The English translation is from volume IX of the second series of *Nicene and Post-Nicene Fathers*, edited by Schaff and Wace (28 vols.; Buffalo and New York, 1886-1900), p. 143 f; hereafter cited as *NPNF*).

[75]*De Trinitate* XII, 55-57 (*PL* 10, 472). (The English translation is from *NPNF* IX, p. 233).

[76]See F. Homes Dudden, *The Life and Times of St. Ambrose* (2 vols.; London, 1935), II, 575.

ρευσις."⁷⁷ There is, however, one text which certainly implies the procession of the Spirit from the Father and the Son.

> Observe now that just as the Father is the Fountain of Life, so, too, *many* have declared that the Son also is signified as the Fountain of Life, because, He says, with You, Almighty God, your Son is the Fountain of Life, that is, the Fountain of the Holy Spirit, since the Spirit is the Life . . . Yet *many* wish that the Father alone be indicated in this passage by Fountain, although they see what Scripture has said. It says: "With thee is the Fountain of life," that is, with the Father is the Son, for the Word is with God. . . .⁷⁸

Since the Carolingian theologians made no distinction between the eternal procession and the temporal mission of the Holy Spirit, it is not difficult to see how easily they could appeal to Ambrose. And, it is quite possible that Ambrose, in fact, would have supported a *Filioque* position.

What is impossible to assess is Ambrose's influence on Augustine concerning this problem. Since Ambrose uses the expression "from the Father and the Son" without stipulating that he is referring to the temporal mission of the Holy Spirit, it is quite possible that Augustine heard him use such expressions often in his sermons.

Augustine

The theological authority for the Carolingian theologians is Augustine (354-430), whose influence on Latin triadology was simply enormous. Augustine not only explicitly teaches the procession of the Spirit from both the Father and the Son, but also gave a certain philosophical perspective to

---

⁷⁷Swete, *op. cit.*, p. 121.

⁷⁸*De Spiritu Sancto* I, 152-154 (*PL* 16, 769). (The English translation is from volume 44 of the *Fathers of the Church,* edited by Schopp (New York, 1947 ff.), p. 90).

trinitarian thought in which the *Filioque* found philosophical support, although self-contradictory.

When Augustine was still a presbyter, he gave a discourse on the Creed before a Council of North African Bishops in 393 which has been preserved in his *De fide et Symbolo*.[79] In the ninth chapter of this book Augustine treats the section of the Nicene Creed—not the Nicene-Constantinopolitan Creed—which confesses "And in the Holy Spirit."

After explaining the analogies used by Tertullian, though not mentioning Tertullian, Augustine states that "these corporeal examples have been given not because they bear any real resemblance to the divine nature, but because they show the unity of visible things, and to let you understand that it is possible for three things not only severally but also together to be designated by a singular noun...."[80]

Although "great and learned commentators of the divine Scriptures have not as yet discussed the doctrine of the Holy Spirit" with precision and fulness, Augustine claims that there are various "schools of thought" concerning the doctrine of the Holy Spirit.[81] However, Augustine clearly states that the Spirit does not derive his existence from himself, for "that would be to set up two independent principles instead of one, which is utterly false and absurd."[82] This remark is quite noteworthy because the Greek East later accuses Augustine of setting up two principles in the Godhead.

Although Augustine states that there are those "who have even dared to believe that the Holy Spirit is the communion or deity, so to speak, of the Father and the Son,"[83]

---

[79]*PL* 40, 181-196. (The English translation is from volume VI of *The Library of Christian Classics*, edited by Baillie, McNeill, and Van Dusen (26 vols.; Philadelphia, 1953), pp. 353-369; hereafter cited as *LCC*).

[80]*De fide et Symbolo* IX, 17. (English translation from *LCC* V, p. 362).

[81]*De fide et Symbolo* IX, 19. (*LCC* V, p. 364).

[82]*Ibid.*

[83]*Marius Victorinus* had referred to the Holy Spirit as the *connexio* or *copula* of the Father and the Son. See Paul Henry, "The *Adversus Arium* of Marius Victorinus: The First Systematic Exposition of the Doctrine of

it is clear that Augustine himself is fond of this idea, discussing it with sympathy in *De fide et Symbolo* and later returning to the idea in *De Trinitate*. According to this view, the Holy Spirit is the mutual love of the Father and the Son, implying that the Spirit proceeds from both of them.

The single most influential work on Carolingian triadology was Augustine's *De Trinitate* (400-416).[84] Although it is true that many of the Carolingians simply quote at length from *De Trinitate*, Ratramnus of Corbie had truly assimilated the contents of the entire work.

In his *De Trinitate* Augustine is moved by the philosophical notion of God as an absolutely simple essence. "He is . . . without doubt a substance, or . . . an essence, which the Greeks call οὐσία. . . ."[85] Moved by his notion of Divine essential simplicity, he identifies all the forms and aspects of Divine existence with essence, ultimately absorbing all these forms into an absolute simplicity. In the Divine existence there is no difference between being and possessing justice, wisdom or power.[86] In God truth is essence,[87] life is essence,[88] and love is essence.[89] At one point Augustine reduces approximately twelve Divine attributes to three, and then

---

the Trinity," *Journal of Theological Studies*, I (April, 1950), 42-55. That Augustine knew the works of Marius Victorinus and his Latin translations of Greek texts has been convincingly argued by Paul Henry. See also Pierre Courcelle, *Late Latin Writers and their Greek Sources*, trans. from the French by H. Wedeck (Cambridge: Harvard University Press, 1969), pp. 173-182.

[84] All page references to the Latin text of *De Trinitate* are from volumes 15 and 16 of *Oeuvres de Saint Augustin*, edited by Agaësse, S. J. and Moingt, S J. (Paris, 1955). (The English translation is from *NPNF* III and follows the reference to the Latin text).

[85] *De Trinitate* V, 2, 3 (15, p. 428; p. 88).

[86] *De Trinitate* VI, 4, 6 (15, p. 480; p. 100).

[87] *De Trinitate* VII, 1, 2 (15, p. 512; p. 106).

[88] *De Trinitate* XV, 5, 7 (16, p. 436; p. 202).

[89] *De Trinitate* XV, 19, 37 (16, p. 524; p. 220).

these three are reduced to one—wisdom, which in turn is identical to essence.[90]

Beginning with and concentrating on the Divine essence, Augustine finds difficulty when he turns to explain the personal life of the Holy Trinity. In fact, he admits that he cannot find an adequate conception of person.[91] "When the question is asked, What three? human language labors altogether under great poverty of speech. The answer, however, is given three 'persons' not that it might be completely spoken, but that it might not be left wholly unspoken."[92] Instead of working within the totality of Christian experience, Augustine too readily adopts a philosophical notion—the Aristotelian category of relation. Persons, he concludes, must be eternal relations; they are called "persons" according to relation.[93] For Augustine, existence is not in itself personal, for whatever is personal in the Divinity is not absolute but relative.[94] Person is *ad se* identical to essence. Person becomes merely another aspect of existence; for God to exist is the same as to be Person, just as it is the same to be good, just, and wise.[95]

At one point Augustine refers to *the* "person of that Trinity"[96] and at another point he asks: "since the three are together One God, why not also one Person...."[97] It is clear in which direction Augustine is inclined—he would like to consider "person" as a common element in the Divine nature, reducible to essence. In his given system "person" is *ad se* a

---

[90] *De Trinitate* XV, 6, 9 (16, p. 440 and 442; p. 203); XV, 17, 27-28 (16, pp. 500-504; pp. 215-216).

[91] See the article by A. C. Lloyd, "On Augustine's Concept of Person," in *Augustine: A Collection of Critical Essays,* ed. by R. A. Markus (New York: Doubleday, 1972), pp. 191-205.

[92] *De Trinitate* V, 9, 10 (15, p. 448; p. 92).

[93] *De Trinitate* V, 5, 6 (15, p. 434; p. 89).

[94] *De Trinitate* VII, 2, 3 (15, p. 514 f.; p. 107).

[95] *De Trinitate* VII, 6, 11 (15, p. 540; p. 111).

[96] *De Trinitate* II, 10, 18 (15, p. 228; p. 46).

[97] *De Trinitate* VII, 4, 8 (15, p. 532; 110).

common element, but he would like also to reduce the relative aspect to a common element. Precisely what stops him is his faithfulness to Tradition.

> It is lawful through the mere necessity of speaking and reasoning to say three persons, not because Scripture says it, but because Scripture does not contradict it; whereas, if we were to say three Gods, Scripture would contradict it....[98] What therefore remains, except that we confess that these terms sprang from the necessity of speaking.[99]

Thus the relative aspect of the Trinity must remain, not because of philosophical necessity, but because of Tradition. Nevertheless, *ad se* the persons are a common element: "... whenever each is singly spoken of ... then they are one."[100]

Everything in God, the persons *ad se* included, is identical to the Divine essence.[101] Augustine states that "it is absurd to speak relatively of substance, for everything subsists in proportion to itself; God more than any other thing."[102] However, an inconsistency arises at this point. If existence is identical to essence, then what type of existence can have "personal relations" if those persons are not already the essence about which one cannot speak relatively?

What is quite interesting is that Augustine's triadology finds no subject in God, certainly not in God the Father, who has no absolute existence, for he is real only in relation to the Son. "If ... then there is something in Him as it were in a subject, and He is not simple ... but it is an impiety to say that God subsists, and it is a subject in relation to His own goodness...."[103] When Augustine uses language which

---

[98]*De Trinitate* VII, 4, 8 (15, p. 532; p. 110).

[99]*De Trinitate* VII, 4, 9 (15, p. 534; p. 110).

[100]*De Trinitate* VIII, preface (16, p. 24; p. 115).

[101]*De Trinitate* V, 5, 6 (15, p. 434; p. 89); VI, 1-3 (15, pp. 468-478; pp. 97-99); IX, 5, 8 (16, p. 88; pp. 128-129); X, 11, 18 (16, p. 155 and 156; p. 142).

[102]*De Trinitate* VII, 4, 9 (15, p. 536; p. 111).

[103]*De Trinitate* VII, 5, 10 (15, p. 536 and 538; p. 111).

The Patristic Background

demands a reference to a subject, then that subject is the simple nature. He writes that the "life which is God perceives and understands...."[104] But life, for Augustine, is identical to essence. He himself writes that the "single nature perceives as it understands."[105] All of this becomes axiomatic with the Carolingian theologians.

Nevertheless Augustine is forced to do something with the fact of Christian tradition—that God is revealed as one being, as the Father, as the Son, and as the Holy Spirit. Augustine thinks that the best way to elucidate the doctrine of the Holy Trinity is by the dialectic of psychological analogies.

Augustine's dialectic takes many forms. The most suggestive and richest, if he had spent more time with it and developed it in another direction, is that of love. He discovers three elements in love: the lover, the beloved, and love itself.[106] But in the final analysis Augustine's analogy of love seems to do serious harm to the Christian doctrine of the Divine Triad. The Father and the Son love each other reciprocally and the Holy Spirit is the expression of this love. Although Augustine does not seem to be aware of it, he has given the Holy Spirit an inferior role, excluding him from the very act of love.

Most of Augustine's other analogies restrict themselves to the structure of *mens* as an image of the Holy Trinity. The mind is considered as "the knowledge whereby the mind knows itself, and the love whereby it loves both itself and its knowledge of itself,"[107] as "memory, intelligence, and will,"[108] as knowledge, faith, and wisdom,[109] as ability, knowl-

---

[104]*De Trinitate* XV, 5, 7 (16, p. 434 and 436; p. 202).
[105]*Ibid.*
[106]*De Trinitate* IX, 2, 2 (16, p. 76; p. 126).
[107]*De Trinitate* XV, 3, 5 (16, p. 426; p. 201).
[108]*De Trinitate* IX, 11-12 (16, p. 104 and 106; p. 132 and 133); XIV, 2, 4 (16, p. 350; p. 184); XIV, 10-12 (16, pp. 382-388; pp. 190-192).
[109]*Ibid.*

edge, and use,¹¹⁰ and as being, knowledge, and life.¹¹¹ Although Augustine's dialectic takes many forms, there are always four basic elements:

1) *essentia*—about which the dialectic is.
2) *essentia*—manifesting itself (the Father).
3) *essentia*—as manifested (the Son).
4) *essentia*—uniting that which manifests itself with that which is manifested (the Holy Spirit), or the expression of the unity of that which manifests itself with that which is manifested.

The last three (the Father, the Son, and the Holy Spirit) are identical to the first (*essentia*). Since God is by *essence* everything; that is, being, nature, spirit, mind, knowledge, truth, love, power and will, an inevitable question arises: why any manifestation at all? Why must the Divine essence manifest to itself what it is essentially? In the logics of Augustine's dialectic manifestation seems not only superfluous but also impossible.

Within this context Augustine develops his doctrine of the relations of the Divine persons and his doctrine of *Filioque*, which is philosophically implied in his dialectic. Augustine writes that "the Father is the beginning of the whole divinity...."¹¹² The Father is the fulness of the Deity because he is *ad se* identical to the essence. The Son and the Spirit are also the fulness of the Deity because they are also *ad se* identical to the same essence; relatively, of course, they are said to derive the essence from the Father."¹¹³ In reality, however, the Father is the principle of the Holy Trinity only relatively: "He is called the Father in relation to the Son, the Beginning in relation to all things, which are from Him."¹¹⁴ For Augustine the Father, Son and the Holy Spirit

---

¹¹⁰*De Trinitate* X, 11, 17 (16, p. 152; p. 142).

¹¹¹*De Trinitate* VI, 10, 11 (15, p. 496; p. 102).

¹¹²*De Trinitate* IV, 20, 29 (15, p. 414; p. 85).

¹¹³*De Trinitate* VII, 6, 11 (15, p. 542; p. 111 and 112); XV, 7, 12 (16, p. 448; p. 205).

¹¹⁴*De Trinitate* V, 13, 14 (15, p. 454; p. 94).

The Patristic Background

are identical in terms of wisdom and knowledge, and yet he identifies the Father with wisdom, knowledge, and memory.[115]

The Son of God is Son relatively; he is the manifestation of the essence which manifests itself and he is united to the principle of manifestation by that which unites, or expresses the already existing unity of (the Holy Spirit) the principle of manifestation with the manifestation. In Augustine's triadology there is no "reason" for the *Logos*, for the relative origin of the Son is from the nature of God. Augustine writes that persons have the power of transmitting to the proceeding persons the Divine essence, but he also writes that person is identical to essence. Whether Augustine approves or not, he ultimately conceives of the processions as "substantial" relations which is diametrically opposed to his idea of the absolute simplicity of the Divine existence. In fact, Augustine even condemns the idea that the essential properties could have different aspects in each of the Divine persons.[116]

Augustine states that the Holy Spirit proceeds "principally" from the Father: "... God the Father alone is He from whom the Word is born, and from whom the Holy Spirit principally proceeds."[117] But he immediately adds: "and therefore I have added the word principally, because we find that the Holy Spirit proceeds from the Son also."[118] In the final analysis Augustine's doctrine is the *Filioque:* "neither can we say that the Holy Spirit does not also proceed from the Son, for the same Spirit is not without reason said to be the Spirit both of the Father and of the Son."[119]

---

[115] *De Trinitate* VII, 2-3 (15, p. 514 f.; pp. 107-108); IX, 11, 16 (16, p. 104; p. 132); IX, 12, 18 (16, p. 108 f.; p. 113); XV, 10, 19 (16, p. 468 f.; p. 209).

[116] *De Trinitate* VI, 1, 2 (15, p. 470; p. 105); VI, 2, 3 (15, p. 472; p. 107); VI, 4-6 (15, pp. 480-488; pp. 109-111); IX, 4, 6 (16, p. 84; p. 128); XV, 7, 11-12 (16, pp. 446-452; pp. 204-205).

[117] *De Trinitate* XV, 17, 29 (16, p. 504; p. 216).

[118] *De Trinitate* XV, 17, 29 (16, p. 504; p. 216).

[119] *De Trinitate* IV, 20, 29 (15, p. 412; p. 84).

Augustine's doctrine of *Filioque* follows logically from his entire perspective of God. Greek patristic thought began with the principle that there is God and He is God the Father. Augustine begins with the principle that there is God and in him there is Fatherhood. On a trinitarian basis it is impossible to reduce the idea of Father to that of "having a Son" because the Father is also the source of the existence of the Holy Spirit. In its widest meaning Fatherhood is best understood as source.

Augustine's support for his doctrine of *Filioque* will be repeated again and again by the Carolingian theologians. First, he reasons that since the Spirit is "of the Son," he proceeds from the Son. Secondly, since the Spirit is sent by the Son, he must therefore proceed from him.[120] Thirdly, since Christ breathed the Spirit on the disciples, the Holy Spirit must proceed from him. Fourthly, since the Holy Spirit is the common bond, the union of love, between the Father and the Son, he must therefore proceed from both. Fifthly, the Father has given the "gift" of the power of *spiration* to to the Son and therefore the Holy Spirit proceeds *as existing* from the son also.[121] The Carolingians use these arguments as well as some of their own in their attack on Byzantine triadology. Photius' response to the Carolingian position is essentially a response to Augustine.

In his *Tractatus in Joannis Evangelium* (c. 416) Augustine presents the question of the *Filioque* openly: "Some may ask whether the Holy Spirit proceeds also from the Son."[122] His answer is quite explicit. "Why should we not believe that the Holy Spirit proceeds also from the Son, since he is the Spirit of the Son also."[123] Augustine argues that Christ would not have breathed the Holy Spirit on his

---

[120]Eastern Christian theology, never denying that the Spirit is sent by the Son, distinguishes between the "eternal procession" and the "temporal mission" of the Holy Spirit.

[121]*De Trinitate* XV, 26, 45 (16, p. 546; p. 224).

[122]PL 35, 1888 ff.

[123]*Ibid*.

The Patristic Background

disciples, if the Spirit did not proceed from him: "What else did that breathing signify except that the Holy Spirit proceeds also from him?"[124]

In this work Augustine also considers an explanation of Christ's words that the Spirit proceeds from the Father. "If, then, the Holy Spirit proceeds from both the Father and the Son, why did the Son say 'he proceeds from the Father'?"[125] Augustine answers by appealing to the humility of Christ; that is, Christ always referred everything that belonged to him to the Father. Augustine asks one to consider whether Christ's statement that "My doctrine is not Mine, but His that sent me?"[126] should be taken literally.

> If, then, it is here understood to be his doctrine, regardless of the fact that he said it is not his, but the Father's—how much more must we then understand the Holy Spirit to proceed from him also, where, speaking of the Spirit "proceeding from the Father," he is careful not to say "he does not proceed from me?"[127]

In this work Augustine is also quite explicit about the simultaneous procession of the Holy Spirit from the Father and the Son: "The Holy Spirit does not proceed from the Father into the Son, and from the Son to the creatures . . . but he proceeds at once from both."[128] Augustine stresses, however, that it is the gift of the Father to the Son that the Spirit proceed also from the Son. These same ideas are later expressed in Augustine's *Contra Maximinum Arianum*.[129]

Thus, the greatest of the Latin Fathers had structured an entire philosophy of the Trinity which implicitly and explicitly taught the *Filioque*. When the Carolingian theologians appeal to Augustine, their appeal is most authentic; there is no problem about spurius texts or about interpretations of the text of Augustine.

---

[124]*Ibid*.
[125]*Ibid*.; the reference is to John 15:26.
[126]John 5:16.
[127]*Tractatus in Joannis Evangelium* 8 (*op. cit.*).
[128]*Ibid*.
[129]*PL* 42, 770.

Bibliography

PRIMARY SOURCES

[The following primary sources come from four source editions: 1) J. D. Mansi. *Sacrorum conciliorum nova et amplissima collectio.* Florence and Venice, 1759 ff.; cited as Mansi in the bibliographic entry; 2) J. P. Migne. *Patrologia Latina.* Paris, 1844-1855; cited as *PL* in the bibliographic entry; 3) J. P. Migne. *Patrologia Graeca.* Paris, 1857-1866; cited as *PG* in the bibliographic entry; and 4) *Monumenta Germaniae Historica;* cited as *MGH* in the bibliographic entry. The sources are primarily arranged in chronological order].

Libri Carolini sive Caroli Magni Capitulare de Imaginibus. Edited by Hubert Bastgen. (*MGH, Legum Sectio III, Concilia Tomi II Supplementum.* Hanover and Leipzig, 1924; p. 110 ff.).

POPE HADRIAN'S *Letter to Charlemagne.* (Mansi 13, 759-810).

Council of Friuli (796 or 797). (*PL* 99, 293-296).

ALCUIN. *De Fide sanctae et individuae Trinitatis* (*PL* 101, 13-22).
Letter 60. (*MGH, Epistolae* IV, p. 104).

Letter 95. (Ibid., p. 139).
Letter 96. (Ibid., p. 140).
Letter 98. (Ibid., p. 142).
Letter 139. (Ibid., p. 220).

Letter of the Pilgrim Monks. (PL 129, 1257-1260).

POPE LEO'S *Letter to the Eastern Churches.* (PL 102, 1030-1032).

THEODULF OF ORLEANS. *De Spiritu Sancto.* (PL 105, 239-276).

Libellus de Processione Spiritus Sancti. (PL 105, 273).

SMARAGDUS' *Letter to Pope Leo III.* (PL 98, 923-929).

Acta Collationis Romae. (PL 102, 971-976).

PHOTIUS. *Encyclical to the Eastern Thrones.* (PG 102, 721-741).

POPE NICHOLAS' *Letter to Hincmar.* (MGH, *Epistolae* VI, 601-609).

HINCMAR'S *Letter to Odo of Beauvais.* (PL 126, 93-94).

AENEAS OF PARIS. *Liber adversus Graecos.* (PL 121, 683-721).

RATRAMNUS OF CORBIE. *Contra Graecorum Opposita Romanam Ecclesiam infamantium.* (PL 121, 223-304).

Council of Worms (868). (PL 119, 1201-1212).

Council of Constantinople (879-880), sixth and seventh sessions (Mansi 17, 511-523).

POPE JOHN'S *Letter to Photius.* (Mansi 17, 523 and 526).

PHOTIUS. *Letter to the Patriarch of Aquileia.* (PG 102, 794-822).

Mystagogia. (PG 102, 279-392).

SECONDARY SOURCES

[The following is only a *select bibliography*]
I. *THE THEOLOGICAL BACKGROUND*

ALTANER, B. "Augustinus in der griechischen Kirche bis auf Photius." *Historisches Jahrbuch*, LXXI (1951), 37-76.

BOLOTOV, V. V. "Thesen über das *'Filioque'* von einem russischen Theologen." *Revue Internationale de Théologie*, VI (1898), 681-712.

BURN, A. E. *The Athanasian Creed*. London, 1918.

CAMELOT, R. P. "La tradition latine sur la procession du Saint-Esprit *'a Filio'* ou *'ab utroque'*." *Russie et Chrétienté*, IV, no. 3 and 4 (July-December, 1950), 211-218.

CHEVALIER, IRENEE. *Augustin et la pensée grecque: les relations trinitaires*. Fribourg, 1940.

CLEMENT, O. "Gregoire de Chypre: 'De l'ekporèse du Saint-Esprit'." *Istina*, no. 3 and 4 (July-December, 1972), 443-456.

COURCELLE, PIERRE. *Late Latin Writers and their Greek Sources*. Translated from French by Harry E. Wedeck. Cambridge: Harvard University Press, 1969.

DE REGNON, THEODORE. *Études de Théologie positive sur la Sainte Trinité*. 3 vols. Paris: Retaux, 1892-1898.

DONDAINE, H.-F. "La théologie latine de la procession du Sainte-Esprit." *Russie et Chrétienté*, IV, no. 3 and 4 (July-December, 1950), 211-218.

DU ROY, OLIVIER. *L'intelligence de la Foi en la Trinité selon Saint Augustin*. Paris, 1966.

EVERY, GEORGE. *Misunderstandings between East and West*. Richmond, Va.: John Knox Press, 1966.

FFOULKES, EDMUND. *An Historical Account of the Addition of the Filioque to the Creed of the West.* London, 1872.

FORTMAN, EDMUND J. *The Triune God.* London and Philadelphia: The Westminster Press, 1972.

GRUMEL, V. "Le *Filioque* au Concile Photien de 879-880." *Échos d'Orient*, XXIX (1930), 257-264.

——————. "Le Décret du Synode Photien de 879-880 sur le Symbole de Foi." *Échos d'Orient*, XXXVII (1938), 357-372.

HEATH, R. G. "The Western Schism of the Franks and the 'Filioque'." *Journal of Ecclesiastical History*, XXIII, no. 2 (April, 1972), 97-113.

HEFELE-LECLERCQ. *Histoires des Conciles.* Tome III, deuxième partie and Tome IV, première partie and deuxième partie. Paris, 1910-1911.

HENRY, PAUL. "On Some Implications of the '*Ex Patre Filioque Tanquam Ab Uno Principio*'." *Eastern Churches Quarterly*, VII, no. 2 (1948), 16-31.

——————. "The *Adversus Arium* of Marinus Victorinus: The First Systematic Exposition of the Doctrine of the Trinity." *Journal of Theological Studies*, I (April, 1950), 42-55.

HERGENRÖTHER, JOSEF. *Photius: Patriarch von Konstantinopel.* 3 vols. (originally published in 1867 in Regensburg) Darmstadt: Wissenschaftliche Buchgesellschaft, 1966 reprint.

JONES, H. W. *The Holy Spirit in the Mediaeval Church.* London, 1922.

JUGIE, MARTIN. *De Processione Spiritus Sancti ex Fontibus Revelationis et secundum Orientales Dissidentes.* Rome, 1936.

KELLY, J. N. D. *Early Christian Creeds,* London, 1950.

——————. *The Athanasian Creed.* London, 1964.

LLOYD, A. C. "On Augustine's Concept of a Person." *Augus-*

tine: *A Collection of Critical Essays*. Edited by R. A. Markus. New York: Doubleday Anchor, 1972, pp. 191-205.

LOSSKY, VLADIMIR. "The Procession of the Holy Spirit in Orthodox Triadology." *Eastern Churches Quarterly*, VII, no. 2 (1948), 31-53.

———. *The Mystical Theology of the Eastern Church*. London, 1957, pp. 44-66; 81-82; 156-173; 240-244.

MARTLAND, T. R. "A Study of Cappadocian and Augustinian Trinitarian Methodology." *Anglican Theological Review*, XLVII, no. 3 (July, 1965), 252-263.

MEYENDORFF, John. "At the Sources of the Filioque Quarrel." *Orthodox Thought*, IX (Paris, 1953), 114-137. (In Russian).

———. "La procession du Saint-Esprit chez les Pères orientaux." *Russie et Chrétienté*, IV, no. 3 and 4 (July-December, 1950), 158-178.

———. *A Study of Gregory Palamas*. Translated by George Lawrence. London, 1964, pp. 228-232.

PERI, VITTORIO. "Il simbolo epigrafico di S. Leone III nelle basiliche Romane dei SS. Pietro e Paolo." *Rivista di Archeologia Christiana*, XLV (1969), 191-221.

PRESTIGE, G. L. *God in Patristic Thought*. London, 1964.

RICHEY, THOMAS. *The Nicene Creed and the Filioque*. New York, 1884.

RODZIANKO, VLADIMIR. "The '*Filioque*' Dispute and Its Importance." *Eastern Churches Quarterly*, X, no. 4 (1953), 177-191.

———. " '*Filioque*' in Patristic Thought." *Studia Patristica* II. Berlin, 1957, pp. 295-308.

SCHINDLER, ALFRED. *Wort und Analogie in Augustins Trinitätslehre*. Tübingen, 1965.

SHERRARD, PHILIP. *The Greek East and the Latin West: A Study in Christian Tradition.* Oxford, 1959.

STEINACKER, H. "Die römische Kirche und die griechischen Sprachkenntnisse des Frühmittelalters." *Mitteilungen des Instituts für österreichische Geschichtsforschung,* LXII (Innsbruck, 1954), 28-66.

SWETE, H. B. *On the History of the Procession of the Holy Spirit.* Cambridge, 1876.

——————. *The Holy Spirit in the Ancient Church.* London, 1912.

VERHOVSKOY, SERGE. "La procession du Saint-Esprit d'après la triadologie orthodoxe." *Russie et Chrétienté,* IV, no. 3 and 4 (July-December, 1950), 197-210.

WOLFSON, H. A. *The Philosophy of the Church Fathers.* Cambridge: Harvard University Press, 1964.

II. THE HISTORICAL BACKGROUND

AMANN, É. *L'Époque carolingienne.* Vol. VI: *Histoire de l'Église.* Edited by Fliche and Martin. Paris, 1941.

BISCHOFF, B., ed. *Das Geistige Leben.* Vol. II: *Karl der Grosse: Lebenswerk und Nachleben.* Düsseldorf, 1965.

BURY, J. B. *A History of the Eastern Roman Empire: 802-867.* New York; reprinted in 1965.

CUISSARD, C. *Théodulfe, évêque d'Orléans.* Orléans, 1892.

DIEHL, CHARLES. *Byzantium: Greatness and Decline.* Translated from French by Naomi Walford. New Brunswick, N. J.: Rutgers University Press, 1957.

——————. *Byzantine Empresses.* Translated from French by H. Bell and T. de Kerpely. London, 1964.

DUCHESNE, L. *The Beginnings of the Temporal Sovereignty of the Popes.* Translated from French by A. H. Matthew. London, 1907.

DUCKETT, E. S. *Alcuin, Friend of Charlemagne*. New York, 1951.
———. *Carolingian Portraits: A Study in the Ninth Century*. Michigan: Ann Arbor paperback, 1969.

DVORNIK, FRANCIS. *The Photian Schism*. Cambridge: Cambridge University Press, 1948.
———. *Byzantine Missions among the Slavs*. New Brunswick, N. J.: Rutgers University Press, 1970.
———. "Byzantium, Rome, the Franks and the Christianization of the Southern Slavs." *Cyrillo-Methodiana: zur Frühgeschichte des Christentums bei den Slaven*. Edited by Hellmann, Olesch, Stasiewski, Zagiba. Köln, 1964.

ELLARD, GERALD. *Master Alcuin, Liturgist*. Chicago, 1956.

FREEMAN, ANN. "Theodulf of Orléans and the *Libri Carolini*." *Speculum*, XXXII (1957), 663-705.
———. "Further Studies in the *Libri Carolini*." *Speculum*, XL (1971), 203-289.
———. "Further Studies in the *Libri Carolini*." *Speculum*, XLVI (1971), 597-612.

GASKOIN, G. J. B. *Alcuin: His Life and His Work*. New York: Russell & Russell reprint, 1966; originally published in 1904.

GIANNONI, CARL. *Paulinus II: Patriarch von Aquileia*. Wien, 1896.

HAENDLER, GERT. *Epochen Karolingischer Theologie*. Berlin, 1958.

HAUCK, ALBERT. *Kirchengeschichte Deutschlands*. Vols. II and III. Leipzig, 1900.

JENKINS, ROMILLY. *Byzantium: The Imperial Centuries*. New York: Random House, Vintage paperback, 1969.

KLEINCLAUSZ, ARTHUR. *Alcuin*. Paris, 1948.

LAISTNER, M. L. W. *Thought and Letters in Western Europe: 500-900*. London, 1931.

LEVISON, W. *England and the Continent in the Eighth Century*. Oxford, 1946.

MANN, HORACE K. *The Lives of the Popes*. Vols. I and II. London, 1925.

OBOLENSKY, DMITRI. *The Byzantine Commonwealth*. New York, 1971.

——————————. *Byzantium and the Slavs*. London: Variorum Reprints, 1971.

OSTROGORSKY, GEORGE. *History of the Byzantine State*. Translated from German by Joan Hussey. New Brunswick, N. J.: Rutgers University Press, 1957.

RZEHULKA, E. *Theodulf, Bischof von Orleans*. Breslau, 1875.

SCHUBERT, HANS VON. *Geschichte der christlichen Kirche im Frühmittelalter*.Tübingen, 1921.

VASILIEV, A. A. *History of the Byzantine Empire*. 2 vols. Madison, Wisconsin, 1961.

WALLACH, LUITPOLD. *Alcuin and Charlemagne: Studies in Carolingian History and Literature. New York,* 1959.

WEST, A. F. *Alcuin and the Rise of Christian Schools*. New York: Greenwood Press reprint, 1969; originally published in 1892.

WOLFF, PHILIP. *The Awakening of Europe*. Translated from French by Anne Carter. Baltimore: Penguin paperback, 1968.

ZAGIBA, FRANZ. "Die Missionierung der Slaven aus 'Welschland' (Patriarchat Aquileja) im 8. und 9. Jahrhundert." *Cyrillo-Methodiana: zur Frühgeschichte des Christentums bei den Slaven*. Edited by Hellmann, Olesch, Stasiewski, Zagiba. Köln, 1964.

List of Roman Popes
[5th - 9th centuries]

Hormisdas	514-523
John I	523-526
Felix III [IV]	526-530
Boniface II	530-532
John II	533-535
Agapetus I	535-536
Silverius	536-538
Vigilius	538-555
Pelagius I	556-561
John III	561-574
Benedict I	575-579
Pelagius II	579-590
Gregory I	590-604
Sabinianus	604-606
Boniface III	607
Boniface IV	608-615
Deusdedit	615-618
Boniface V	619-625
Honorius I	625-638
Severinus	638-640
John IV	640-642
Theodore I	642-649
Martin I	649-655

Eugenius I	655-657
Vitalian	657-672
Adeodatus	672-676
Donus	676-678
Agatho	678-681
Leo II	682-683
Benedict II	684-685
John V	685-686
Conon	686-687
Sergius I	687-701
John VI	701-705
John VII	705-707
Sisinnius	708
Constantine	708-715
Gregory II	715-731
Gregory III	731-741
Zacharius	741-752
Stephen II	752
Stephen II [III]	752-757
Paul I	757-767
Constantine	767-768
Stephen III [IV]	768-772
Hadrian I	772-795
Leo III	795-816
Stephen IV [V]	816-817
Paschal I	817-824
Eugenius II	824-827
Valentine	827
Gregory IV	827-844
Sergius II	844-847
Leo IV	847-855
Anastasius	855
Benedict III	855-858
Nicholas I	858-867
Hadrian II	867-872
John VIII	872-882
Martin II [Marinus I]	882-884
Hadrian III	884-885

Lists of Patriarchs of Constantinople
[6th - 9th centuries]

Timothy I	511-518
John II	518-520
Epiphanius	520-535
Anthimus I	535-536
Menas	536-552
Eutychius	552-565
John III	566-577
Eutychius	577-582
John IV	582-595
Cyriacus I	595-606
Thomas I	607-610
Sergius I	610-638
Pyrrhus	638-641
Paul II	641-652
Pyrrhus	651-652
Peter	652-664
Thomas II	665-668
John V	668-674
Constantine I	674-676
Theodore I	676-678
George I	678-683
Theodore I	683-686
Paul III	686-693

Callinicus I	693-705
Cyrus	705-711
John VI	711-715
Germanus I	715-730
Anastasius	730-754
Constantine II	754-766
Nicetas I	766-780
Paul IV	780-784
Tarasius	784-806
Nicephorus I	806-815
Theodotus I	815-821
Antony I	821-832
John VII	832-842
Methodius I	842-846
Ignatius	846-858
Photius	858-867
Ignatius	867-878
Photius	878-886
Stephen I	**886-893**

List of Roman (Byzantine) Emperors
[6th - 10th centuries]

Justinian I	527-565
Justin II	565-578
Tiberius I	578-582
Maurice	582-602
Phocas	602-610
Heraclius	610-641
Constantine III	641
Heracleon [Heraclonas]	641
Constans II	641-668
Constantine IV	668-685
Justinian II	685-695
Leontius	695-698
Tiberius II	698-705
Justinian II [second time]	705-711
Philippicus Bardanes	711-713
Anastasius II	713-715
Theodosius III	715-717
Leo III	717-741
Constantine V	741-775
Leo IV	775-780
Constantine VI	780-797
Irene [Empress]	797-802
Nicephorus I	802-811

Stauracius	811
Michael I	811-813
Leo V	813-820
Michael II	820-829
Theophilus	829-842
Michael III	842-867
Basil I	867-886
Leo VI	886-912
Alexander	912-913
Constantine VII	913-959

List of German "Roman" Emperors
[9th century]

Charlemagne [Rex Francorum, 768]	800-814
Louis the Pious	814-840
Lothaire	840-855
Louis II [in Italy]	855-875
Charles II, the Bald [West Franks]	875-877
Charles III, the Fat [East Franks]	881-887
Interregnum	888-891

Index

Abelard, Peter, 89
Ado of Vienne, 41
Adoptionism, 49, 53, 55
Aeneas of Paris, 101, *103-107*, 108, 167, 170
Agnellus of Ravenna, 24, 71, 106
Aistulf, 39, 40
Alcuin, 30, 34, 35, 48, 59, *60-62*, 69, 72, 92, 107, 168
Ambrose, 15, 16, 47, 71, 75, 81, 106, 118, 153, 179, 185, *195-196*
Anastasius Bibliothecarius, 89, 124
Angilbert, 46
Apologists, 179-181
Arianism, 27, 49, 110, 117, 118, 161, 180, 181, 182
Aristotle, 119, 199
Athanasius, 15, 19, 20, 21, 26, 47, 73, 74, 75, 81, 98, 106, 118
Athanasian Creed, 21, 26, 53, 58, 68, 71, 76, 118, 160, 185
Augustine of Canterbury, 31
Augustine of Hippo, 14, 15, 16, 17, 19, 23, 24, 26, 35, 36, 43, 47, 51, 52, 58, 60, 61, 62, 70, 71, 72, 73, 75, 76, 77, 81, 106, 112, 115, 119, 120, 136, 137, 148, 151, 153, 159, 160, 165, 168, 176, 179, 185, *196-205*.
Autchar, Duke, 39
Avitus of Vienne, 24

Basil the Great, 47, 75, 98, 153, *187-189*.

Bede, Venerable, 30
Benedict, 68
Boethius, 24
Boris of Bulgaria, 92, 93, 101, 124.

Caesar Bardas, 93
Caesarius of Arles, 27
Cappadocian Fathers, 17-19, *187-189*
Cassiodorus, 24, 71, 106
Charlemagne, 40, 45, 46, 48, 53, 55, 59, 61, 63, 66, 67, 69, 79, 91, 92, 166
Childebert, 41
Clovis, 41, 42

COUNCILS:

A] *Ecumenical Councils*

First Ecumenical [Council of Nicaea, 325], 25, 26, 28, 46, 50, 56, 94, 115, 116, 126, 127, 160, 162, 163, 165, 166, 167, 197
Second Ecumenical [Council of Constantinople, 381], 25, 26, 28, 29, 43, 46, 47, 48, 56, 94, 106, 115, 116, 117, 126, 127, 153, 160, 162, 163, 165, 166, 167
Third Ecumenical [Council of Ephesus, 431], 25, 28, 74, 75, 163, 197
Fourth Ecumenical [Council of Chalcedon, 451], 26, 28, 50, 74, 77, 83, 106, 132, 154, 156, 163
Fifth Ecumenical [Council of Constantinople II, 553], 74, 75, 83, 137, 154, 165
Sixth Ecumenical [Council of Constantinople III, 681], 48, 83, 94, 95, 96, 154, 167
Seventh Ecumenical [Council of Nicaea II, 787], 45, 46, 47, 48, 128, 130

B] *Non-Ecumenical Councils*

Council of Aachen (809), 69, 79, 80, 81
Council of Braga (675), 29

Index

Council of Constantinople (867), 99, 102
Council of Constantinople [Anti-Photian] (869-870), 125, 126
Council of Constantinople (879-880), *123-130*, 138, 151, 155, 171, 172
Council of Florence (1438-1439), 188
Council of Frankfurt (794) 52, 53, 55, 57, 59, 163, 164
Council of Friuli (796/797), *55-59,* 131, 163
Council of Gangra (mid-4th century), 96
Council of Gentilly (767), *41-44*
Council of Hatfield (680), 30
Lateran Council (649), 33
Council of Lyons (1274), 14
Council of Merida (663), 29
Council of Milan (680), 31
Quinisext Council (692), 94, 95, 96, 172
Council of Rome (680), 31
Council of Rome (863), 126
Council of Rome (869), 126
Council of Sardica (343), 95
Council of Toledo (589), 27-29, 160
Councils of Toledo (633; 638; 655; 675; 681; 683; 688; 693; 694), 29
Council of Valence (855), 14
Council of Worms (868), 103, 120, 121, 168, 170
Cyprian, 35
Cyril of Alexandria, 14, 19, 33, 47, 71, 74, 75, 81, 106, 179, *189-194.*

Dagobert, 41
Didymus, 15, 71, 106, 118, 179, 185, *186-187,* 188
Dionysius of Alexandria, 153
Droctegang, Abbot, 39

Egilbald, Georg, 63
Einhard, 41, 45
Elipandus, 55

EMPERORS:

Emp. Anastasius (491-518), 41
Emp. Basil I (867-886), 93, 108, 110, 120, 123, 124, 125, 126
Emp. Constantine V (741-775), 38, 41, 92
Emp. Constantine VI (780-797), 45
Emp. Constantine VII Porphyrogenitus (913-959), 91
Emp. Heraclius (610-641), 41, 91
Empress Irene (797-802), 45, 46
Emp. Justinian I (527-565), 76, 77
Emp. Leo III (717-741), 37, 38
Emp. Leo VI (886-912), 125, 141
Emp. Maurice (582-602), 38, 41
Emp. Michael I (811-813), 92
Emp. Michael III (842-867), 108, 110, 120
Emp. Nicephorus (802-811), 92

Eucherius of Lyons, 24
Eugenius, Papal Legate, 127, 155
Eusebius of Caesaria, 185

Faustus of Riez, 24
Felix, 55
Flavian, 74
Formosus of Porto, 93
Fulgentius Ferrandus, 24
Fulgentius of Ruspe, 24, 71, 72, 73, 106, 118

Gennadius of Marseilles, 24, 118
Gondowald, 41
Gregory of Nazianzus, 15, 47, 72, 73, 98, 118, 179, 187-189
Gregory of Nyssa, 47, 75, 187-189
Gregory of Tours, 42

Hadrian of Africa, 31
Harun al-Rashid, 63
Hilary of Poitiers, 15, 16, 47, 71, 75, 106, 179, 194-195

Hincmar of Rheims, 101, 102, 103, 164, 170
Hippolytus, 150

Ibas of Edessa, 76, 77
Iconoclasm, 37, 38, 39, 41, 42, 46, 161
Irenaeus, 153
Isidore of Seville, 27, 29, 52, 71, 106, 162

Jerome, 35, 71, 72, 106, 186, 187
John Cassian, 35
John Chrysostom, 75, 98
John Damascene, 18
John Scotus Eriugena, 14, 34
Julianus Pomerius, 24, 106

Leander, 27
Libri Carolini, 42-53
Liutbert of Mainz, 103
Louis the German, 93
Louis the II, 99

Macedonianism, 27, 98, 147
Marcellus of Ancyra, 185
Marinus, Priest, 32
Marius Victorinus, 197, 198
Maximus the Confessor, 32, 33
Methodius, 153
Michael Syncellus, 168
Mocianus, 76
Modalism, 180, 181
Monophysitism, 76
Monothelitism, 31, 32

Nestorianism, 76
Nestorius, 74, 193

Odo of Beauvais, 103
Origen, 180

Palladius of Grado, 131
Paschasius, Deacon of Rome, 24, 118

PATRIARCHS OF CONSTANTINOPLE:

Patriarch Ignatius, 123, 124, 125
Patriarch Nestorius, 74
Patriarch Photius, 14, 36, 38, 43, 50, 90, 92, 93, 94, 95, 96,
　　97, 98, 99, 101, 104, 105, 107, 109, 121, 123, 124, 125,
　　126, 127, 128, 129, 130, 131, 132, 133, 134, 135, 136,
　　137, 138, 139, 141, 142, 143, 144, 145, 146, 147, 148,
　　149, 150, 151, 152, 153-157, 161, 167, 168, 169, 170,
　　171, 172, 173, 174, 175, 176, 177, 191, 202
Patriarch Stephen, 141
Patriarch Tarasius, 46, 47, 48, 133, 162
Patriarch Timothy, 29

Patriarch Thomas of Jerusalem, 69
Paul, Papal Legate, 127, 155
Paul of Populonia, 93
Paulinus of Aquileia, 25, 53, 55-59, 92, 116, 120, 131, 163,
　　164
Pelagius, 36
Peter, Cardinal, 127, 155
Peter Damian, 89
Peter Lombard, 89
Pippin, 39, 40, 41, 161, 162
Pontianus of Carthage, 77

POPES OF ROME:

Pope Agatho, 31, 91, 154
Pope Benedict, 155
Pope Celestine, 74, 153
Pope Damasus, 153
Pope Gelasius, 75

Index 229

Pope Gregory the Great, 25, 31, 35, 47, 66, 71, 80, 81, 106, 118, 154
Pope Gregory II, 37
Pope Gregory III, 37
Pope Hadrian I, 46, 47, 48, 53, 55, 56, 133
Pope Hadrian II, 123, 124
Pope Hadrian III, 155
Pope Honorius I, 91, 92, 105, 167
Pope Hormisdas, 25, 71, 106
Pope John VIII, 125, *128-130*, 131, 138, 155, 172
Pope Leo the Great, 24, 47, 71, 72, 73, 74, 75, 132, 154
Pope Leo III, 40, *64-69*, *79-89*, 106, 107, 129, 132, 133, 154, 155, 161, 164, 165, 166
Pope Leo IV, 155
Pope Martin I, 32, 33
Pope Nicholas I, 41, 93, 94, 95, 99, 101, 102, 103, 105, 108, 119, 120, 121, 164, 167, 170, 172, 173
Pope Paul I, 41, 43
Pope Sergius I, 95
Pope Stephen II (III), 39, 40, 41, 161, 162
Pope Vigilius, 24, 154
Pope Vitalian, 30, 31
Pope Zachary, 154

Praxeas, 181
Priscillianism, 28
Proclus, 71, 75, 106
Prosper, 71, 106
Prudentius, 71, 106

Quinisext, Council, 94, 95, 96

Ratramnus of Corbie, 17, 25, 101, 103, *107-120*, 147, 148, 149, 156, 164, 165, 166, 167, 170, 171, 189, 198
Reccared, King, 27, 28
Regino, Abbot, 41
Richard of St. Victor, 18
Rotrude, 45
Rusticus, Deacon of Rome, 24

Sabellianism, 147, 180, 184
Sabellius, 28
Serapion, 182, 183, 184
Smaragdus, 79-81, 166, 167
Sophronius, 47

Tertullian, 35, 180, 181, 197
Theodoret of Cyrus, 76, 77, 193, 194
Theodorus Lector, 29
Theodore of Mopsuestia, 76
Theodore of Tarsus, 30, 31
Theodulf of Orleans, 29, 48, 69, 70, 71, 79, 104, 106, 162, 163, 166
Theophanes Grapti, 168
Theophilus, 75, 180

Unitarianism, 180

Vigilius of Thapsus, 24, 71, 106, 162
Vincent of Lérins, 27

Walpert of Aquileia, 131

THIS BOOK IS FROM THE
PERSONAL LIBRARY OF
REV. WINSTON F. CRUM, PRIEST
DIOCESE OF MINNESOTA
DIOCESE OF EAST TENNESSEE